BUTTONS ARE TO PUSH

BUTTONS ARE TO PUSH

Developing Your Child's Creativity

MILTON A. YOUNG

PITMAN PUBLISHING CORPORATION

New York   Toronto   London   Tel Aviv

Acknowledgements

"The Answers," from *Forever X*. Copyright 1951, by Robert Clairmont. Reprinted by permission of the author.

"The Child Next Door," from *Fairies and Chimneys*, by Rose Fyleman. Copyright 1918, 1920, by George H. Doran Company. Reprinted by permission of Doubleday & Company, Inc.

"The Wee Bird," from *Young Writers, Young Readers,* rev. ed. 1963, edited by Boris Ford. Reprinted by permission of Fernhill House, Ltd.

"The Sunbeams," from *Miracles*. Copyright © 1966, by Richard Lewis. Reprinted by permission of Simon & Schuster, Inc.

"What's a Boy For?" by Bernard W. Busse, from *Childhood Education*, October 1966, vol. 43, no. 2. Reprinted by permission of Bernard W. Busse and the Association for Childhood Education International, 3615 Wisconsin Avenue, N.W., Washington, D.C. Copyright © 1966 by the Association.

Library of Congress Catalog Card Number: 70–92120
Manufactured in the United States of America
Designed by Michael Olds
1.9 8 7 6 5 4 3 2 1

DEDICATION

Watching children grow is most beautiful. Each new experience has a freshness that is delightful to share with them. When they grow, I grow. Thank you Paul, Susan, and Dara, for being my children, and Ellie, for being my wife. Thanks to all the other children, both grown-up and young, who have shared the thrill and beauty of growing and experiencing with me.

CONTENTS

BUTTONS ARE TO PUSH

THINKING ABOUT THINKING

We are all frequently told to "think," but probably no other word is so often misused, so little understood, and so little practiced. Supposedly, one of the basic differences between man and the other animals is man's ability to reason and to create new ideas. For thousands of years civilizations have become great because of the ability of their members to evaluate their surroundings critically, to solve the problems of their communities, and to create new situations that are better than those that previously existed. Many ancient civilizations (including the Greek, Hebrew, Egyptian, and Chinese) tried to select those young people who appeared to have the most ability to solve problems, and then tried to teach them to use this ability to achieve greatness.

Now, more than ever, it is evident that the future of our civilization depends upon our children's ability to think. Not only will they be called upon to solve the overwhelming problems that face us today, but they must also be prepared to cope with the rapid and constant changes that the future will bring. *The ability to think effectively is the basic element required for coping with change.*

As the world becomes more complex, the demands upon the individual to deal with new and different ideas grow greater. Scientific knowledge has doubled in the past seven years and will probably double again in the next seven. The rapid rate of discovery of new facts and the creation of new materials make it increasingly difficult for youngsters to become completely knowledgeable in even one area, let alone in the entire range of thought. In the past, men like Aristotle and Leonardo da Vinci were able to master all the knowledge in many fields simply because there was a limited amount of information available. Today there are many jobs, such as computer programmer, astronaut, systems engineer, that did not even exist twenty years ago.

When we have helped our children to think effectively, we will have helped them to deal with the mountains of new facts and information that surround them. When children have learned how to go about solving today's problems, they will also have learned to evaluate critically what is presented to them, to select certain elements, to make decisions, and to hold minority opinions that they feel they can defend as right. When we have freed their imagination and rewarded their creativity, we will have taught them to view the world and its problems as challenges to be attacked and overcome rather than passively accepted. When we have helped children to free their emotions and to be sensitive about what happens around them, we will have helped them to find enjoyment in dealing with their environment and in building a positive, creative existence.

From every level of society, every economic group, from educational, political, business, labor, and farm leaders, we hear the constant din that the future depends upon today's children and that they must learn how to cope with the changing environment. Most people who take the trouble to look at the curricula in the public schools are amazed to find that students today are expected to learn many times more information than the students of 20 or 30 years ago. Many of these observers are aware that knowledge of an immense number of facts alone is not sufficient and that, ultimately, it is the skill with which information is used that determines its usefulness and its value. Too many, however, look only at test scores as measures of successful learning. Children who do not learn how to use information in addition to learning facts will find it difficult to compete with others for positions of importance in the society of the future. They will find it increasingly difficult to lead satisfying and fruitful lives.

There are many creative men and women who suggest —even insist—that their own special technique is the only remedy for all learning problems. We have all heard such slogans as "Read the Great Books," "Discipline is the only answer," "Let's go back to phonics," "Study Latin and Greek," and "We must have scholars for teachers" given as the answer to all our ills. There are other adults who feel that the way to improve a youngster's ability to think is to add additional amounts of work to his daily load in school, to extend the school day, or to give more homework. More work and longer hours do not improve a child's learning—nor does change for the sake of change. (How many times have we heard that we need to change the methods used to teach reading?) These simplistic solutions only tend to confuse and divide those who want to make a concerted effort to improve education.

The engineer who refuses to suggest how a building should be constructed without careful analysis of the data, the physician who still may not know the cause of an illness after considerable study, and the lawyer and the businessman who agree that they need years of experience to cope with their everyday problems too often feel that teaching is really a simple task and that anyone can step into the classroom and teach.   Unfortunately, *the simple truth is that there is no single simple truth,* and all the well-meaning people who suggest a particular panacea for helping youngsters learn how to think only hurt the entire effort by stressing a single element.   Although there are some general principles of learning, each child learns differently; a technique that works for one group of children may fail dismally with another group.   Even those who know that the accumulation of information does not, by itself, help children learn to think cannot suggest techniques for teaching children to learn to think.   Very few educators have analyzed the nature of effective thinking and actually tested their theories on children.

We are fortunate in some ways, however, because there is an increasing awareness and concern by parents and schools, and greater efforts are being made to determine how to go about helping youngsters to prepare themselves for the future.

David Russell, Jean Piaget, and others who have studied the conceptual development of young children have found evidence clearly showing that the ability to think through problems, to cope with new situations, and to create new ideas is part of *an ongoing process that children learn from their environment, and one that starts at a very early age.*

Children connect ideas.   For example, Jane says, "You're tired, Mommy. I'll help you wash the dishes," or "I watch the man bring us oil to keep us warm"; Bobby, who jammed his tricycle in a fence by running it over the bottom bar, gets off, goes around, and pushes the bike through from the other side; and Sally pushes a chair over to the sink so she can turn on the water.   No parent who is aware of the tremendous number of changes that will occur throughout his children's lives would willingly deprive these children of the experiences and assistance that they need to handle new situations, new materials, new ideas, and new concepts.

Parents know that, at a very early age, children appear to have a natural curiosity and are wonderfully imaginative.

The Answers

"When did the world begin and how?"
I asked a lamb, a goat, a cow.

"What's it all about and why?"
I asked a hog as he walked by.

"Where will the whole thing end and when?"
I asked a duck, a goose, a hen.

And I copied all the answers too,
A quack, a honk, an oink, a moo.

Robert Clairmont

This curiosity and imagination appears to form the basis of the child's ability to think effectively later on in life. Most children want to know why things happen, how things work, what makes things go, how things are related to each other, and a multitude of other facts. "What are you looking for?" Mother asks little Bobby as he crawls behind the TV. Bobby answers the question with one of his own. "Where are the people in the TV?" Or he may ask, "Mommy, how do you know what's inside a can?" or "What makes a telephone talk?" Children are not usually interested in lengthy explanations, even when parents know the answers. Parents encourage thinking by helping the child think the answer through. Of course, the answer depends upon the age and sophistication of the child. It is important to help the child understand, but it is also important not to underestimate his knowledge and give him obvious, oversimplified answers. A simple acknowledgment of the question and a short encouraging response such as "That's a good question," or "Let's find out," is better than "That's too complicated for you to under-

stand," or "Don't bother me now; can't you see I'm busy?"
or "Go ask Daddy." Even when these queries come hundreds
at a time in a constant stream, parents and teachers must
avoid killing the child's curiosity and his ability to imagine.

The Child Next Door

The child next door has a wreath on her hat;
Her afternoon frock sticks out like that;
All soft and frilly;
She doesn't believe in fairies at all
(She told me over the garden wall)—
She thinks they're silly.

The child next door has a watch of her own;
She has shiny hair and her name is Joan;
(Mine's only Mary).
But doesn't it seem very sad to you
To think she never her whole life through
Has seen a fairy?

Rose Fyleman

WHAT KIND OF THINKING ARE WE THINKING ABOUT?

"Shhh, I'm thinking about what I'd do if I could have all the toys in the store." "I don't know why, but I think what you are doing is wrong." "I was thinking of our last visit." It is apparent that we are "thinking" all the time. That is, thoughts are continuously running through our minds. Asleep or awake we are "thinking." There are many ways to consider thinking and many ways to define the word. David Russell suggests that it be divided into two broad general categories. The first category we may call random thinking, or *nondirectional thinking*. This type of thinking is going on much of the time. The quotations at the beginning of this paragraph are clear examples of nondirectional thinking. They are merely reflections, ideas, or thoughts passing through the mind. The person is not really concentrating on his thoughts and they are not going in any particular direction.

When you remember an incident that happened when Aunt Jane visited you last summer, reminisce about the golf game that you played last weekend, or express some idea that is not intended to go in any particular direction, you are involved in nondirectional thinking. The same kind of thinking occurs when you lie on a beach with stray, unrelated thoughts running through your mind, when you notice a flower, or when you see a pretty picture of someone you recognize. Though you are always aware of many elements in your environment and constantly receive impressions through your senses, you do not *consciously* think of all of these impressions; you select only the ones that you feel are important at a particular time or those that are called to your attention.

In some instances, a particular incident or picture causes random associations in your mind. Leaves falling from a tree may remind you of a long walk you once took through the woods or that you have to rake the lawn. The squeal of car brakes reminds you of an accident that almost happened last week or last month. Certain things are randomly associated in your mind, while other things remind you and connect things you remember—but still with no particular direction to your thoughts. This is nondirectional thinking.

The second broad category of thinking may be called *directional thinking,* and it is this type that will be dealt with throughout this book. Directional thinking may be referred to as "thinking effectively," "effective thinking," or sometimes just "thinking." *This is the kind of thinking that occurs when our thoughts are moving us toward a solution or a goal.*

We may be drawing a conclusion, forming an opinion, or deciding if we will do something later in the day. We may be solving a problem, determining if something will work, judging, inferring, deducing, reasoning, estimating, critically evaluating a situation, or creating a new idea. It is not always necessary that we actually arrive at the solution or that we reach a decision as long as the thinking is moving in the direction of a solution.

The housewife trying to decide what to purchase for tomorrow's supper is doing directional thinking. She may not come to any definite conclusion. Perhaps she feels that she needs more information before settling on the menu. She may want to check the newspaper to see what is on sale, ask her husband what time he will be home, or consider what the children would like. Then she may actually decide what to buy.

The same kind of thinking occurs when we evaluate the speech of a political candidate. There are certain aspects of it that we may like or dislike; we may agree with parts of it and disagree with others. However, we need not decide whether to vote for that candidate until we have listened to more of his statements or heard what the opposing candidates have to say.

Directional thinking occurs *even before a decision is made*. When a new thought occurs to us, we examine it and test the idea in our minds, searching for problems and ramifications. When a child organizes a game in some new way or uses a toy in a manner that is different from its purpose, or when an adult makes use of a particular piece of equipment in a novel way—this thinking is directional.

Sometimes we may become aware of a particular problem and attempt to solve it. Even if we do not succeed, we are engaged in directional thinking. "I saw the man make a penny disappear," Johnny shouts out. "I'm going to do it, too."

"I saw it! I saw it!" sister Jill exclaims, pointing to his pocket.

"Let me try again. You won't see it this time." Attempts to solve the problem represent directional thinking, even though the solution may take Johnny years. For very young children, directional thinking may involve simply deciding which toy to play with and which one to let another child play with, or how to get a particular toy out of the cabinet when it is in an awkward position. When children learn to evaluate their own ideas, they begin to think critically about ideas expressed by others; thus they become involved in another level of directional thinking.

Finally, creative endeavors are included in the scope of directional thinking. Alison was so engaged when she wrote

The wee bird
Creeping up the tree
Never even heard
Or saw me.

So was Linda, when she wrote

Sun, Sun, do you know
You are beams in the flame,
With glow worms
And bright yellow red,
Sharp silver flame
Spinning up,
Like a big block of gold.
The sun is a very magic fellow.

In his book *Education for Effective Thinking,* William H. Burton suggests that, in general, thinking is directional when it moves toward a goal or conclusion, and that it occurs in three main areas: problem solving, critical thinking (or evaluation), and creative thinking.

It is obvious that all of us are thinking (or may be thinking) on several levels at the same time. Starting with non-directional thinking, we may wander into recognizing a problem, and then turn to directional thinking to try to solve the problem. Perhaps we can think about the same idea on non-directional and directional levels at the same time. Or we may shift back and forth between levels. We may notice a new car driving by, be pleased by the color, compare it to last year's model, and note the people in it (nondirectional); then we may shift to thinking about the problem of getting a new car, how to finance it, and the type of car to get (directional); and then we may go back to noticing the color of the passing car's seat covers (nondirectional).

Nondirectional thinking, as we described it at the beginning of this section, is extremely important because it often serves as a basis for directional thinking. Parents can help children improve in nondirectional as well as in directional thinking. We realize that we do not actually know what is occurring inside the human brain at a specific point and time; we do not really know which connections are open or how to open them, how systems sort out conflicting information, how things are put together in concepts and images, or how these concepts and images are extracted and utilized when needed. Nor do we know how people having the same experiences seem to perceive or see them in different ways. Until the time comes when we know exactly how people think, we must help our children on the basis of what we can see them doing and what we have learned about the way other children behave.

Curiosity and Imagination

An understanding of what we mean by curiosity and imagination is also important to our discussion. If human beings were not curious and did not use their imagination to create things and to solve problems, we would not have most of the things that we accept as a normal part of our life today. Both learning to use fire and splitting the atom resulted from man's curiosity. Curiosity seems to appear in all children at an early age, and it forms an important basis for learning. It shows itself as eagerness for information, as inquisitiveness and questioning, as interest in new ideas and things, as a desire to explore. Curiosity is an important motivation for learning and for effective thinking. You can see curiosity operating in the little child as he tastes his new teddy bear, examines the mechanism of a toy, forms his blocks into new patterns, pulls on a tablecloth, or stares intently at a shiny object.

"Let's play make-believe," Jane tells her Daddy.

"Okay, tell me how to play it," says Dad.

"Make believe I'm an octopus and could squeeze you with eight arms instead of two. How would you feel?"

"Four times as wonderful," replies Dad.

Fantasy, originality, imagery, illusion, inventiveness, and improvisation—all these are involved in imagination. Though it actually means the power of the mind to create new images, it has also come to mean the ability to conceive new ideas, or see things in a new light.

A five-year-old reported, "I love the wind; it goes fast and slow and you can see it even though it's invisible." Some authorities contend that children imagine that things are different from what they really are, or think of things in an unusual way, because they lack the knowledge or skill to see things as we adults really know they are. Others believe that children have good imaginations because their thinking, unlike an adult's, is not inhibited by knowledge, experience, and prejudice. Whichever school of thought is correct, we must attempt to preserve in our children their ability to imagine things in unusual ways. The major breakthrough scientific discoveries were made by people like Albert Einstein, who retained his ability to be unimpressed and uninhibited by the fact that something appeared impossible.

If we crush a child's curiosity and train him in such a way that he feels that questioning, investigating, and searching are bad, we have virtually doomed him to being a non-thinker when he grows up. Keeping alive a youngster's curiosity and encouraging his imagination may make life much more difficult for his parents (because of a constant barrage of questions and ideas), but such parents are giving their child an essential base for a future of effective thinking.

Problem-Solving Behavior

Problem solving is one of the aspects of directional thinking. "Mommy, I have a problem," states three-year-old Jane as she stands in front of her mother.

"What's your problem?" asks Mother with an interested look.

"There is no toilet tissue in the bathroom and I have to go," states the young lady in a firm manner.

"Well, what do you think might be the answer to your problem?" asks Mother, who has trained herself to let her child solve problems.

"Should I get some more from the closet?" Jane asks rhetorically as she moves off to solve her own problem.

Obviously, problems vary in difficulty from situation to situation. Unfortunately, the word "problem" is often used to describe questions that are not really problems, since the answer is clearly known to the person asking the questions. Often we find teachers and parents asking children questions—but calling them problems. These children are not really being asked to solve problems: They are being asked to recall things they have learned and repeat them in response to questions. How many times have we seen the following?

> Problems to be answered:
> What is the sum of 4 apples and 4 apples?
> What occurs when subset A intersects subset B?
> What is the capital of Bolivia?
> What countries won in World War I?
> What is the object of the sentence?
> What is the formula for water?

These are not problems. They are questions that demand answers based on memorization and recall. We will avoid using the terms "problem" and "problem solving" in that sense. Russell suggests that those situations that simply require recall be called *tasks*. These include "a job to be done," "a fact to be remembered," or "elements to be interpreted."

Following a recipe to bake a cake is not solving a problem but performing a task. Knowing who was in command of a particular army in a particular year is recalling a fact. Listing a textbook's reasons for the outcome of a battle is also just remembering facts, and not problem solving. Manipulating things that one already knows toward a solution that has already been thought through is not a problem but a task.

Essential to problem solving are (1) information or background, and (2) a method to solve the problem. When we present a problem to a child who has no way of knowing how to start solving the problem and does not have enough information to suggest even *possible* solutions, we are presenting him not with a problem but with a puzzle. His approach will tend to be by trial and error, and he will probably have no way of evaluating whether his approach is a good one or not.

Problem solving can be used only in situations where the person has the information (or knows how to find the information) and the ability to find an answer, and where the solution is unknown. Try working with children on problems when you do not know the solution, so that you can learn with them.

A child who had visited a residential center for older people told her group in school about the visit. She talked about the old people having little to do but watch TV. The youngsters became quite involved in the story and a great sadness fell over them. "Can we do anything to help?" one little boy asked. "Let's ask our teacher." By recognizing that a problem existed, the children were taking the first step toward solving it. They were thinking directionally.

Critical Thinking

The ability to evaluate the elements in one's environment is also an important part of directional or effective thinking. "Do those people on the television always tell the truth, Daddy?" little Raymond asked his father.

"What do you mean by that, Ray?" replied his father, wondering what the boy was leading up to.

"Well, just now a man said that Nutty Oats taste just like real nuts, and that's not true because the other day Mommy bought me some and I tasted them and I don't think they taste like real nuts at all." It is important that children learn to evaluate what they hear and read so that they can make decisions based upon the evidence.

Critical thinking, by definition, involves recognizing that there may be ideas other than the one presented, and also being able to select the important elements of the situation or statement. It also includes weighing the elements suggested and using reason to move toward a decision. It is clear that the success of our form of government depends on the ability of each citizen to evaluate ideas and to think critically. Decisions based upon critical analysis of the events that determine our very existence are made daily by our leaders. Today, controversial problems confront us to a much greater extent than ever before in the history of the world. We play a role in their eventual solution.

Critical thinking is definitely related to both problem solving and creative thinking; all have elements of the others. Often, problem-solving ability is necessary to take a situation to the point where critical thinking may be applied.

Creative Thinking

What makes a person creative? What are his characteristics? Among the qualities found in creative people are sensitivity to problems, fluency of ideas, flexibility, and originality. They have the ability to rearrange and redefine their ideas, and they are willing to defer judgment. Some writers claim that the term "creativity" has been distorted and no longer has a pure meaning.

While this may be true, we have chosen to define creative thinking or acts as they relate to the individual as well as to the group.

A creative person is one who through his own efforts succeeds in doing something that is new or different for him.

A child who utilizes a toy in a new way is performing a creative act on the simplest level.

> *I jump*
> *My shadow jumps with me*
> *I sit and think about myself*
> *What does my shadow think about?*

At the next level, an individual may create something new or different for the larger group. Finally, there are those few people, such as Copernicus, Freud, and Einstein, who create whole new media, concepts, or fields of thought.

It is more important that we provide the environment and the kind of experiences that will produce creative acts on any level than that we discuss endlessly whether or not we should define the term in a restrictive manner.

IS THINKING REALLY VALUED IN OUR CULTURE?

In spite of the evident need in our society for imaginative, creative, and thinking people, and in spite of the lip service given to the idea that children should be taught to think effectively, our society sets itself directly against thinking individuals in almost all areas of our daily lives. There are many examples of this unfortunate and hypocritical situation. The "organization man" is allowed to think as long as he follows the company line. As soon as he deviates by creating original ideas, he is out of line, discouraged, and sometimes out of a job. Those who have attempted to get a really different idea or system accepted by a committee, a group, an organization, or a government agency probably know the odds against new and imaginative innovations.

The schools give us another example of how extremely difficult it is to change an established pattern. Instead of investigating how children learn and what they need to know, schools often pretend to be changing when they are simply beefing up the curriculum by making it more difficult. More material is introduced into earlier grades (so that achievement test scores are higher) and more hours of work are added (to keep children out of the parents' way). Education is too often the mere passing on of knowledge, rather than the teaching of problem-solving behavior. In spite of all the superficial changes, the teacher is usually lord and master of a space between four walls that is filled with chairs, desks, and children in pretty much the same way as it was at the turn of the century. Increasingly, there seems to be a major emphasis on "getting your kid into the best college." Many parents are so anxious to have their children achieve this goal that they do not see that high grades do not mean that their children have obtained an education that will enable them to function as contributing members of society.

Television programs constantly emphasize the idea that there is only one solution to a problem, that a character is either right or wrong. It is rare indeed for a problem to be presented from various points of view, and rarer still for a program to indicate that all questions may not be answered with a simple Yes or No. Very, very seldom does a program suggest that all acts need not be all right or all wrong, or that there may be a number of solutions to a problem—and sometimes none.

In general, society does not support independent thinking, and schools reflect this attitude. Young adults and teenagers are admonished to stick to the straight and narrow path. "Keep your nose clean, don't try anything too new, do what you are told, and you'll be accepted and receive your just reward." Teachers are frequently like their students and do as they are told by the school administrators.

People who ask too many questions are considered troublemakers and are not tolerated in many organizations. Many teachers and other adults who start out being imaginative and creative soon learn that it is wise to keep quiet. Some find a recreational outlet for their creative abilities and others change their jobs, but too many just accept the situation and learn to fit into a pattern.

Each of us is a guardian of our own right to think freely. We *must* support efforts to help children retain their curiosity and imagination and to think creatively—but perhaps those of us who are concerned with effective thinking are asking too much of others. Do we have the right to work at keeping curiosity alive in our children and at encouraging imagination and effective thinking? For, with the ability to think comes understanding and concern about the problems that confront us and will confront future generations. With concern comes a feeling of responsibility and a need to act. Is it right for us to help people recognize that there are problems, or to help them feel that they can act to solve them? Would it be better for us to let our children continue being like most children in the past, denying them the opportunities and experiences that could help them learn to think effectively and live creatively? Perhaps the age-old habit of wearing blinders is better for most people, with thinking left to an elite corps of people who will think and solve the problems for everyone. Many civilizations have operated under this philosophy and it exists in many countries today.

Many of us cannot accept the concept of "elite thinkers." We feel that those who have not retained the ability to be creative and to think effectively miss many of the joys of living. We feel that the future of our civilization depends upon the ability of more people to be able to reason and to think. It is our belief that the more successful we are in helping children to remain curious and imaginative, the more effectively children develop their ability to think and the greater is our hope for survival and improvement.

This book is based upon the author's belief that effective thinking is essential. Since a child's early years are crucial to sustaining this ability, parents and teachers have a grave responsibility to create the proper environment and to provide the necessary experiences. If we fail, we will be responsible for locking future generations into prisons of their own minds, and probably giving civilization a push on the road to its own destruction.

What's a Boy For?

Why, a boy is for becoming a man,
For building his dreams as best he can,
For searching in each day some new way
His strength and skill to display,
To hunt with brave men he can find
Any time within his mind,
And share the fleeting kiss of fame
With more of heroes than he can name,
Now with dragons spitting fire,
Now with men in space attire,
Laughing and shouting, and yelling with glee,
Running or tumbling, or climbing a tree,
Chasing a squirrel or petting a dog,
Feeling the eerie mystery of fog,
Seeking new ways to be what he must
Before he yet must return to dust.

Bernard W. Busse

Probably the first question that we have to ask ourselves is, "Do we, as adults, think effectively?" Most of us believe that we do think and that we have effective methods for problem solving, that we are critically evaluating our everyday environment, and that we create new ways of handling situations and new ideas in the face of new problems.

Learning together with your own children can be a stimulating enterprise. As part of this, there are a number of questions that you can ask yourself about your own thinking. It is probably true that you who are reading this book think more effectively than those who would not be interested. You probably already have an advantage. The very fact that you are thinking about thinking; that you are curious about how effective thinking can be taught; that you are concerned with your children's future and their ability to face a changing world—all this indicates that you are critically evaluating current situations and those of the future.

If you are a person who enjoys a problem, enjoys working through a solution, and feels satisfaction when a solution is found, you can probably help your children by showing them how you do your own problem solving. If you are the type of person who reads editorials in the newspaper, who sends a letter to the editor, or who reacts to a political speaker wondering about more than his appeal for higher taxes, then you are probably a person who is critically evaluating his environment. If you are constantly testing your actions and checking to see if you are being unjust to others; if you have thought about the values you believe in and consciously utilize these values in working with others; if you stand up and are counted even in an unpopular cause; then you are the type of person who critically evaluates a good deal of his environment. If you change your views as new evidence is presented, and if you do not believe that *everything* was better in the good old days or that complicated problems can be solved with simple solutions, then you have the flexibility that is required to operate creatively.

If you love to go into a new situation and disregard what has been done before, preferring to try a solution of your own, you are functioning in a creative manner and your children are probably learning this from you. If you are fortunate enough to have the imagination and intelligence and freedom to create really new ideas or new materials, then your creative ability is greater than most, and, with a little effort, you can help your children learn to use their talents.

The point is this: The more effective your own thinking, the more successful you will be in helping your children think.

DO YOU WANT A CHILD
WHO THINKS EFFECTIVELY?

Jimmy sits quietly when he goes to the shoe store. He is a very good student in school. He does all his work very well. He is well behaved. He knows the answers to all the teacher's questions. He likes to play with his toys and to run about and play with other children. His table manners are frequently commended by others. He usually listens and does as he is told. He goes to bed on time, etc., etc., etc.

Billy has his problems. He can't sit quietly all the time. He likes to explore new things. Whether you want him to or not, he will constantly bombard you with questions. His success with tasks, both at home and at school, varies greatly, from outstanding to negligible. His interest leaps from one thing to another. For a time, he is intensely interested in some things and completely lackadaisical about others, and then, unpredictably, he changes. He sometimes makes up stories— and believes them. He frequently doesn't get along with his friends and is often not even interested in playing with them. His behavior at the table frequently leaves a great deal to be desired. He may not always accept things you say as correct.

It is easy to understand the appeal of the child in the first paragraph, for he is much easier to deal with, and is potentially a good organization man. Training such a child is relatively simple: Inhibit his behavior, make him follow instructions, and require that he believe everything that you, his teacher, and his books tell him.

If, however, you decide to use the information in this book to help your child become an adult who can use his imagination in problem solving—a person who critically evaluates the things that happen around him and who is creative in his approach to life—then you must be prepared for a child who functions more like the child described in the second paragraph. When you encourage a child to use his curiosity and imagination, you are opening up Pandora's box. There is no telling exactly what will come out, but it is possible to make certain predictions. Your child will become more knowledgeable than you in many areas. He will challenge your point of view, sometimes because he disagrees with you and sometimes just for discussion purposes. His interests will range far and wide. He will seek to be independent in what he does. He will have ideas that seem farfetched to you. He will make demands of your time and attention and, at times, he will be difficult to live with. The difficulties will be many, but the rewards will be greater; you will have the tremendous satisfaction of raising a child full of uninhibited enthusiasm, fresh ideas, and the joy of learning on his own.

PARENTS HAVE A CHOICE

Young children have a great deal of natural curiosity. They are constantly examining their environment—both mentally and physically. They like to touch things, and to smell them and taste them. They like to play with blocks, to build, to saw, and to hammer. They are curious about nature and are interested in animals, flowers, bugs, and rocks. They like to paint and color. They like music. They like to listen to stories and to "read" the pictures in books.

With so much going on in the child's experience, parents have an extremely important role to play. In most instances, parents determine just how long a child's curiosity will last, how much imagination he will retain, and how creative he will become. Too often, because it takes time to answer a question, or because we do not want to be bothered, we destroy a great deal of the child's curiosity and imagination—the qualities upon which he builds his capacity to think effectively.

Parents have a choice. They can give their children the experiences that will help them grow into thinking, creative adults or, through neglect and lack of understanding, they can raise unthinking, dull people.

Some Guidelines

Following are some guidelines for parents who want their children to learn to think effectively. The various points will be discussed in detail in succeeding chapters.

It is not sufficient merely to tell children to "think." They need to be encouraged to think and to formulate and present their own problems.

When a child feels that a problem is important to him, he really wants to try to solve it. There must be strong motivation for a youngster to succeed in problem solving. If your child thinks he has a problem, accept it as one, even if you don't agree.

All children start out with an active imagination and intense curiosity about what goes on around them. You should nurture this imagination and curiosity. They are the foundations of effective thinking.

You need to be careful in judging the difficulty of problems before presenting them to children, so that you strike a balance between problems that are too simple and those that are too difficult.

Parents who give children solutions to problems—rather than helping them to think them through—are teaching the youngsters that solutions can be found by using outside resources. Children need to be encouraged to think through and solve their own problems.

It is important to realize that, although you cannot and should not yield to youngsters' questions and demands all the time, you must commit yourself to helping a youngster solve his problems as often as possible.

Children must first understand the problem before they can begin to solve it. Lack of understanding turns a problem into a puzzle.

Although children will bring you many problems and explore their environment on their own, you should, in addition, broaden the horizons of the children's world and point out elements in situations that will motivate them to solve problems and to develop their own ideas.

If you let a youngster assist you in establishing rules for a particular situation, he will not only gain insight into the problems of the particular situation, but will learn to handle other situations where rules need to be applied. A willingness to solve new problems appears to carry over.

Children can be encouraged to evaluate their *own* ideas and techniques in solving problems. Help should be available when necessary, but it is usually wiser to wait until a child asks for help before stepping in.

Sometimes, children need time to think about things before they can try to solve them.

Guidance in how and where to search for solutions is

important for youngsters, especially as problem areas become more difficult.

As children get older, they can be taught to analyze situations critically through actual practice. Having children test their solutions by actually trying them out is probably the best way to teach them that it is essential to think situations through to their conclusions before settling on a solution. Learning when to suspend judgment is important in thinking critically or in solving problems.

The more organized the concept, the easier it is to use the available material in problem solving. Thus, learning how to organize helps in solving problems.

Critical thinking starts at an early age. You can encourage young children to develop this ability by verbalizing your own critical analysis of things.

Creative activity occurs on an elementary level in even very young children. Reward and encouragement keeps the creative spark alive.

Fantasies, wishes, and dreams seem to play an important part in developing imagination and, therefore, in developing the ability to think. When children express these fantasies, they are not intentionally lying.

Youngsters think imaginatively in many different ways. You should not try to set a pattern for your child or for other children. Controlling imagination tends to deaden it.

Helping youngsters to sense things in their environment and to be stimulated by them will build their ability to think creatively later on, for it has been found that adults who work creatively have the ability to perceive and integrate factors in their environment.

Children often react spontaneously to situations. Spontaneity, an important element in creativity and imagination, should be encouraged.

Children need to feel free to be imaginative and creative. A child should be given freedom to experiment with his environment as well as with his own ideas.

Positive parental attitudes toward children's questions encourage thinking.

Listening to what children say encourages their creative self-expression.

New situations and new experiences help children to become aware of and sensitive to the stimuli that surround them. Making resources available to children, so that they feel encouraged to use them, leads to their learning how to find needed information.

Fostering a constructive attitude toward what a child sees, hears, and reads teaches reliance and belief in self.

Emphasizing the process rather than the end product encourages imaginative solutions.

Examples of the thinking process and emphasis on open-endedness suggest to children that there are many possible solutions and not necessarily only one.

THE CHILD'S WORLD

"I Want to Go to the Moon."

"Did you hear the jet breaking the sound barrier?" "Ten, nine, eight, seven, six, five, four, three, two, one, blast off!" "We had fun on my TV school."

How different the world is for children now from what it was just twenty or thirty years ago. How different life is for them growing up today, constantly exposed to the tremendous explosion of new ideas. Children living in the twenties and thirties could hardly dream of the experiences that the youngsters of today meet and deal with every day of their lives. Facts about faraway places and about how other people live are brought into their lives on an intimate, personal basis. They are familiar with astronauts, satellites, computers, and electronics, and accept them as commonplace. They do not doubt that they will go to the moon and to the planets and beyond.

"I Think with My Silly Old Brain."

I hear with my ears
I see with my eyes
I smell with my nose
I touch with my hands
I taste with my mouth
And I think with my silly old brain.

Most adults have not really considered the possibility that young children can think. A majority of grownups seems to feel that all they need do is fill a child's mind full of facts, teach him certain skills, and expose him to a random variety of experiences to have him become a successful adult. According to this reasoning, it is unnecessary to be concerned with how children evaluate situations, how they solve problems, and whether or not they learn to think creatively.

The preponderance of evidence obtained by such researchers as Martin Deutsch, J. M. Hunt, and others leads us to conclude that *many of a child's attitudes and concepts are built during his preschool and early school years, and that these provide the framework for later understanding, imagination and creativity.* We are certain now that the early period is vitally important as a period of forming attitudes toward learning and of establishing the concepts to which future experiences can be related. B. S. Bloom studied young children and states, in *Stability and Change in Human Characteristics,* that children learn half of what they will learn during their entire lives by the time they are six years old.

"Show Me the People Inside the TV."

It has become increasingly apparent to researchers, such as Jean Piaget writing in *The Origins of Intelligence in Children* and David Russell in *Children's Thinking,* as well as teachers who work with preschool children, that the ability to think has its roots in early childhood. The overwhelming evidence has led authorities to attach an increasing amount of importance to experiences during the early childhood years, and to the relationship of these experiences to the emotional growth of children and their final behavior as adults. It is unfortunate, however, that so little attention has been paid to the development of the child's curiosity, imagination, and ability to think during these important years.

A young child with a rich background of experiences that challenge his curiosity and imagination will build them into concepts that will aid him to think effectively later on. Too often, we are unconcerned about how and what children learn until they are older; and, even then, we are so busy filling them full of facts and activity that we neglect to teach them how to think effectively.

At two, three, and four years of age, children have already accumulated a vast amount of knowledge. Even during these early years, children are interested in hundreds of topics, and they ask numerous questions related to their immediate environment. While young children may have poor concepts in relation to time, history, distance, and geography, they still persist in asking questions in these areas. "Why is the moon following us?" "Why does smoke go up?" "How do bugs fly?" "What makes the wind blow?" "Do the Russian people like us?" "Why does he talk so funny?" "How high is the sky?" "Where does your lap go when you stand up?" Each response an adult gives is carefully fitted into a concept that is being built in the child's mind.

Children are sometimes naïve in their thinking, and sometimes make funny blunders. A five-year-old told his teacher, "My father is lucky. The policeman gave him a ticket so he can go to the police station free now." However, this incident indicates clearly that the child is thinking effectively, even in a situation where he is making errors. When Billy rushed into his house after school demanding that his mother buy him a set of pistols, holsters, and a gun belt, she inquired why. Billy answered, "The teacher told us that tomorrow we are going to learn to *draw*."

As soon as a baby begins to distinguish among sounds in his environment and to focus his eyes on things around him, he begins to absorb information about his world. He soon becomes aware of the forces that operate on the edges of his world—his mother coming and going, a light, a door, the crib. The infant's earliest learnings are about things that are in his surroundings, and his earliest pleasurable responses usually involve familiar things—his fondness for a particular teddy bear or his joy at taking a bath.

We have all seen a child pick something up and immediately put it into his mouth so that he can taste and feel it. This is one of the early methods of experiencing the outside world. At first, the mother is the center of attention, but quite soon the child is able to interact with other members of the family and, as he grows older, with people in his immediate neighborhood. Children are always trying to understand how to relate to their environment and are constantly testing out these relationships, as trying and difficult as this may be for the adults in their immediate vicinity. Infants will grab at your nose, pull your hair, or eat your collar. Later they spill the soap powder, crawl under your feet, or try to climb the bookcase.

Children are innately curious about how things work— what makes them go, stop, turn around, roll about, or fall down. They ask questions about how the car operates, what makes electricity turn on and off, how the TV works, what makes the sound in the radio, and about countless other mechanical details, attempting to put these working things into a frame of reference for better understanding. "Soda has bubbles," we were told by three-and-a-half-year-old Susan. "It's stuff that tastes like the other food is asleep."

Even before he is three years old, the child attempts to organize his impressions. As soon as children have some idea of their surroundings, they begin to associate ideas. This leads them to construct their first concepts and to make their first contact with abstract thinking. "Who has a birthday next in your house?" inquired four-year-old Jill.

"Junior is next," replied Freddy.

"No." Jill responded, "Junior doesn't count because he is a dog."

"He doesn't have to count," Freddy stated emphatically. "We tell him how old he is."

Kenneth Wann, Professor of Early Childhood Education at Columbia University, writing with some of his associates in *Fostering Intellectual Development in Young Children*, recently recorded 609 different topics as being understood either partially or totally by three-, four-, and five-year-old children. The investigators were continually being surprised at the depth and extent of the information and understanding that these children had. The children had a good deal of confusion about time relationships, but not only were they aware of things in our time and in their immediate environment, but they had information about far distant countries and early history. The researchers were continually impressed, too, at the way this information was being used by the children. Apparently they were constantly looking, searching, and scouting for new materials that they then absorbed into the concepts they had already formed. In our own experience with young children we found instances like these:

Bobby could recount from memory every picture in a storybook. Willy taught Kathy how to count in French. George was found building a ladder so he could reach the ceiling to paste on it the stars he had made. One group of children tried to bring some snow into the room so they could put it on their pictures, while others brought in sand so they could slide on the floor. One child asked the teacher for a penny he had given her several months before. The capacity for remembering the tremendous amount of information they perceived was truly remarkable.

Wann reported that these very young children were found to be using the same techniques for the building of concepts as those used by older children and adults.

(1) They attempted to use the information in a meaningful (although sometimes erroneous) manner.

(2) They were continually testing and readjusting their ideas.

(3) They associated new ideas with those they had, and attempted to make the new ones fit.

(4) They were making generalizations on a number of levels at the same time.

(5) They were working out relations between cause and effect.

(6) They classified new objects and events.

After one observes the actions of young children carefully for any length of time, the above findings do not really seem so amazing. Children get new information when they obtain a new toy to play with or when they have any new experience—Mother takes the child shopping downtown, Daddy repairs a leaky faucet, the child falls and scrapes his knee, a new baby comes to the house, Aunt Martha comes to visit, the family goes to the zoo. In addition, children are affected by the tremendous amount of material that comes through television, radio, and overheard conversations.

"Why didn't you stay under cover during the heavy rain?" Mother asks Richard, who is coming in sopping wet.

"I was already so wet that I thought I would catch a cold if I stopped so I kept on running home so I could get out of the wet clothes." If we are made aware of the process, we can see constant evidence of the children's growing ability to think effectively even though it be erroneous or uneven at times. Children are almost always making critical evaluations and solving minor problems in such activities as choosing sides for a game; finding out which are the best swings to swing on; figuring ways to get their parents to give them something that they want; plotting how to get something they desire from another child; or planning how to climb up a tree. Anyone who has watched a group of children trying to entice a youngster with a new toy into the group must be aware of the volume and complexity of the thinking and problem solving that goes into each ploy.

"If you don't do your homework, you have to take the consequences," Mother scolded.

"Please, Mommy, I don't want any consequences," Martha wailed. So many new words and ideas impinge upon children that it is no wonder that they view the world as something of a puzzle. Think how you would function in an unfamiliar country of giants (which is how we may seem to children) constantly bombarded with ideas you only partially understand in a language only slightly familiar to you.

As information is received, it may be formed into erroneous concepts. Often children have no idea as to how things fit together. Some children do not comprehend the relationship between cows and milk, or between the water they drink and a lake or reservoir. Four-year-old Greta climbed up on the counter to answer the telephone. When the phone fell, she picked it up and said to the caller, "I'm sorry. I hope you didn't get hurt." In spite of this confusion, we find that children obtain, absorb, and use information in a truly remarkable manner. They appear to obtain great satisfaction from obtaining knowledge and information and attempting to use it in play situations.

Children are hunters stalking jungle animals, spacemen taking off in rocket ships, mothers feeding their infants and rocking them to sleep, teachers conducting lessons, or fish swimming in the sea. Acting out situations reinforces their learning and expresses what they have learned. It also builds a sound self-concept. Children use the dramatic play to try out relationships and ideas.

It is important that we pay attention to our children as we walk through the park, sit in a car, or play in the back yard, and that we notice the new information they absorb. Tipping his head up to the sky, a four-year-old said, "Hey, it's like the beach—blue water and white waves." Too often, however, adults are not interested in the things around them and are not aware of this keen interest on the part of children. As parents, we need to feed this curiosity and love for learning so evident in young children. Our own attitude regarding a respect for knowledge and the ability to solve problems sets the tone for our offspring. Children are extremely accurate in imitating the interests and attitudes of their parents and other adults. It is the thinking parent who is concerned about what and how children are learning and who carefully guides a youngster when questions are asked.

Betty (who is six years old) had asked a number of questions regarding her mother's pregnant condition, and Mother had answered them on Betty's level, explaining that the baby was being formed within her and that in nine months the baby would be born. Apparently, Betty had carefully considered these facts for several days because one day she said, "Mother, after the baby is born and the baby has lived for a year, the baby will be one year old. Is that right?"

"Right," said Mother.

"Well," said Betty, looking quizzical, "if the baby was really made nine months before it was born, shouldn't the baby be a year and nine months old?"

Somewhat startled, Mother replied, "That's true, Betty. You know, in some countries they actually count the baby as being nine months old when the baby is born. But in this country the baby is considered as being no years old on the day it is born and a year later it is considered one year old. It's just the way we have of saying things. That was a very good idea you had. I'm proud of you for being able to figure out things like that."

"Honest, Mom, It Was a Real Tiger."

It is sometimes difficult for a child to distinguish between what is real and what is fantasy in his world. Both the actual and the unreal appear the same, and both are real to the child. "Mom! Mom!" Gene called as he ran into the house. "You should see the tiger Mark and I chased out of our back yard."

"Now, Gene," Mother said, "you mean a cat or a dog."

"Honest, Mom, it was a real tiger," Gene protested.

Sometimes children's imaginations play tricks on them. They are sometimes accused of lying when what they have reported they have actually seen in their mind's eye. Sometimes it is difficult to distinguish between what the youngster is really imagining and feels is the truth and what he has conjured up in his imagination to solve a particular problem or avoid a difficult situation. *The ability to imagine and fantasize is an extremely important asset to a young child.* As the youngster grows older, this ability to imagine, combined with information and knowledge, serves as the basis for creative thinking.

The types of fantasies that children have offer a clue to their personality and their growth pattern. There is no doubt that a dangerous situation can develop if the child stays in this fantasy world for extended periods of time. However, serious behavior deviations resulting from fantasies are extremely unusual in the young child.

Prior to the age of three, children seem to find it very difficult to distinguish between the real world and the imaginary world of their dreams. Waking up in the morning, three-year-old Betty asked if she could see her cousin Jean. "Jean lives far, far away," Mother told her.

"No, Mommy, I was just playing with her in our house," Betty replied, insisting that her mother go and find Jean. As the youngster grows older, he begins to differentiate between the real world and the imaginary world. As he attempts to fit new ideas and information into a more realistic set of concepts, his free imagination apparently suffers and his creative ability may actually diminish.

It is important for parents to understand that children need the opportunity to express their fantasies and to work out relationships to reality. Tommy, a four-year-old, once told us, "I'm a rocket ship that goes up and up through the clouds and sky. I'm a spaceman sitting in the captain's chair. Would you like to come with me to Mars?" It is through this acting out that children learn to recognize the difference between ideas they have about the real world and those that belong to the fantasy world. It is sometimes very important for those who are responsible for young children to recognize the need for providing the activities and means for them to express their fantasies. Painting, dramatic play, and working with clay are three activities that help contribute toward the integration of experience that serves as a basis for distinguishing between the real and the fantasy worlds. Children who are deprived of opportunities to act out may sometimes prolong this period and hold on to their dream world for an extended time, or they may become very fearful, conforming individuals with little imagination. It took Dara just a few creative moments to produce this poem:

> The seed I planted in the ground
> Popped out to see the air.
> It grew and grew.
> A tiny flower on the top
> Was all yellow and white.
> It was pretty as can be.
> It is my flower.

"Will You Be My Friend?" (Relationships to Others)

It appears that young children are not able to correct certain errors in the way they behave because, at first, they have no basis for appraising the correctness of their actions. They sometimes behave incorrectly without noticing the error, much to the annoyance of some of the adults and children who are with them. Often, children are simply being spontaneous and enjoying the experiences; they have no notion as to whether they are good or bad, acceptable or unacceptable. Children climb under tables and chairs, touch delicately balanced lamps, rummage through other people's closets, interrupt in a loud voice, demand unobtainable objects, take off their clothes, and use up all the Band-Aids—and they never consider what adults may think of their behavior.

Society, however, insists that children begin to follow its rules at quite an early age. Children are soon made aware of actions that do not conform to adult standards of behavior. Children are rewarded for acting as they should and are punished for violations.

Through his everyday experiences, a child learns how to handle new social situations. Four-year-old Greg and his mother had discussed Aunt Ann, who was very overweight and seemed to exercise very little control where eating was concerned. A few days later, Aunt Ann came to spend the evening, munching chocolates as she talked. Greg suddenly announced, "My mother said you eat too much. That's why you're so fat!"

"Greg, don't say that!" his ten-year-old brother shouted. "That's not nice. Fat people don't like being called fat."

In an infant, the need for socializing is evident when the child cries as his mother leaves the room or when he enjoys having adults play with him. In the next stage of development he plays *alongside* other children. Playing *with* other children begins for some children at the age of two or three. By the age of four, the child has often been convinced that it is good to share, for sharing brings the approval of adults. Also, in many cases, there are dividends in the form of toys shared by the playmate. When we meet a child for the first time he will often ask, "Will you be my friend?" He is beginning to form concepts that help him understand what is demanded of him and what he must do to be a friend. As language develops, he may begin to label social situations. "Play house," "have a party," "cowboys and Indians," and "go visit" are examples of this labeling. In each of these situations, children attempt to utilize information they have in order to solve problems that arise. Children are constantly improving their ability to solve their problems, although errors are sometimes numerous. "May I have that?" asks Jane of her aunt.

"What? Show me what you want," replies her aunt.

"I can't. Mother told me it was not nice to point."

Attitudes toward social behavior are influenced first by early experiences within the family and later by other people who have close contact with the child. In their play, children emulate the behavior of the adults and other children in their environment. "I'll be the father; that's easy, he's always telling everyone what to do," declared Alice.

"I'll be mother and sit outside all day," volunteers Judy.

"I'm the baby," says Susan. "I'll just lie here and play."

"I'm a Giant." (Symbolism)

As you observe the actions of children and listen to their talk, the symbolic nature of their expression becomes clear. "I'm a giant," says Jimmy as he draws himself up taller than the other children. Billy actually looks as if he is taking off as he announces, "I'm a rocket blasting off." Children act out their ideas of reality in a symbolic manner. These actions, which involve thinking out situations, form the basis for more complex thinking later. As children approach the preschool and early school years, their symbolic activities become complex and involved. They demand objects that are more nearly real. It is interesting to note that children can act out situations and verbalize ideas often after merely listening to what someone said or seeing a picture.

"Am I a Good Boy or a Bad Boy?" (There Are Only Absolutes)

Three-year-old Teddy was scolded for tearing a toy dog out of his two-year-old sister's hands. "It's mine," he sobbed, "it's mine." He was not wholly wrong, because it did belong to him.

Young children have not learned that there can be things that are neither wholly right nor wholly wrong. Children try to take off their clothes on the street just as they do at the beach; they find it hard to understand that what is acceptable in one situation is completely wrong in another. Because of the abstract nature of the concepts, gradations of good and bad elude them until they are at least of school age. Most young children will insist on your telling them the absolute truth or giving them a clear-cut response. They assume you know everything, and if you make a mistake they may accuse you of lying. "Is it always wrong to tell a lie?" they wonder. ("If telling a white lie is all right to help someone else, why can't I lie when it helps me?") Everything must be either bad or good, right or wrong, easy or hard.

"I Don't Like the Vacuum Cleaner." (Associations)

Before children learn to organize their experiences, they sometimes rely on ideas that they have associated or linked together to solve problems. For some children, thinking is performed in pairs or short chains of ideas. We can see evidence of associations between ideas quite early in a child's life. Ideas like "food" and "mother" are among the first associations. Later, a child will express some actions through associated ideas— holding out his bottle for more milk or crying to attract attention. The loud noise that is made by a vacuum cleaner may frighten a child and, through association, the child becomes afraid of the vacuum cleaner, whether it is running or not. Too often, children's reactions to situations are based upon their association of emotional reactions. Adult reactions to situations, noises, names, or colors can sometimes be traced to experiences they have had as young children.

It is sometimes difficult to follow a child's thinking, and it is not unusual to find a young child arriving at erroneous conclusions. Billy asks, "Mom, doesn't Daddy like fish?"

"What makes you think that?" Mother answers with another question.

"Well, he's always coming home late on Fridays when we have fish." Billy's father worked late on Fridays, and Billy had erroneously associated the two ideas.

Although children's associations may be faulty and their interest sporadic, the important thing is that they are making associations and are attempting to come to conclusions.

"Why Don't Things Fall Up?" (Questioning)

Questioning is another tool that the child uses to learn how to make associations and build up concepts. After the age of three, a great deal of a child's conversation is in the form of questions. As most parents know, this phase usually reaches its peak during the early school years. At first, the questions are concerned with what things are. Later on, they become questions about why things happen. Boys ask more questions about why things happen, while girls are more concerned with relationships among people. The what-to-why sequence is the usual pattern for children. First the questions are, "What's this? What are you doing? What are these used for? What are clouds made of?" These change to "Why are you doing that? Why are these hers? Why can't I do this? Why can't I have a cloud?"

Parents may impair the child's concept building by ignoring or avoiding his questions ("Don't bother me. Can't you see I'm busy? Talk to me later. Go ask your father. What am I, an encyclopedia? Can't you see Daddy's tired?"). Or, parents may attack the questioner ("That's a stupid question. Don't you know anything? That's silly. What do you want to do that for?"). These are negative replies. However, parents can also cut down the child's learning by giving quick, pat answers ("Yes. No. Always. Cheese. Brown. 1792.") or incomprehensible answers ("That's a conclusion, not a question. The proper elements are combined; it's just a different form, H_2O.'').

If the child is to be helped to build concepts that will enable him to think effectively, the way in which a parent responds to questions becomes critical. When a child asks, "Why don't things fall up?" a poor answer is, "Things can only fall down." Responses to such questions require care and consideration. It takes a great deal more self-discipline to think about what the child is really asking—and to ask for more details before responding—than it does to give an answer simply to silence the child. The response depends on the child's age and interest. It may be better to answer with a question like "Tell me what you are thinking about," and then go on from there.

While some parents deliberately discourage a child from asking questions, others unconsciously discourage questioning by overwhelming the child with the answers. "What makes wood float on water?" Billy asks his father. Father looks up, carefully folds his newspaper, and launches into a discussion of specific gravity, displacement, and the composition of matter. Overwhelmed with detail, Billy loses interest. Two days later when Billy's brother says to him, "Let's ask Dad about the problem," Billy's reply is, "Oh, no. You know what happens. We don't want a two-hour lecture with encyclopedias and stuff. Just forget it." Response to questions is a serious undertaking, and parents must probe carefully to find out just what information the child wants. Parents will be wrong a number of times and correct at other times. It's what they do most of the time that counts.

"Who Am I?" (Self-Concept)

As the child grows older and has contacts with people outside his family, concepts of relationships with others, as well as a picture of himself, are developed. He begins to learn that certain kinds of behavior are expected of him at specified times, and that people accept him or reject him depending upon what they expect of him. He begins to compare himself to others. He may see himself as big or small, strong or weak, fast or slow, or good or bad, depending upon the real or imagined things that happen to him. What might appear as a minor incident to an adult can be very important to a child.

A chance remark ("If Billy weren't sick, we could go to the party," or "It isn't fair to compare him to Jane, with her IQ.") can be deeply disturbing to a child. At an early age, he frequently sees himself only as others see him. How a person feels about himself determines how he looks at the world. If a child feels that he is not wanted, he may work desperately to get people to like him. If he is not noticed, he may do things to gain attention. If he feels unloved, he may try to prove to himself that he is really loved.

Children learn from what parents *do* rather than what they *say* to do. This places a great responsibility on us as parents, because children are quick to notice discrepancies between words and actions. ("Why do you lie and say I'm under six just to get me on the bus free? You told me I shouldn't lie.") Parents who seek to improve their own behavior have a positive effect on their children.

"Daddy, Make the Car Go." (Understanding and Interpretation)

The degree to which children understand and interpret depends a great deal upon the child's personality, upon his maturity level, upon what messages his senses receive (what he sees, hears, smells, tastes, or feels), and upon how his brain *interprets* the images that he receives. Understanding involves not only a child's immediate physical reaction (seeing, hearing, smelling, tasting, or touching), but also his interpretation of previous experiences with similar actions or objects.

Russell has found that children as young as six months old have learned to distinguish shapes. This suggests that they understand the difference between things before they actually learn language. Russell has classified perception in the following ways: form, space, time, movement, weight, numbers, social, athletic, and humor. Since there is a great deal of overlapping among these categories, several may occur at the same time and reinforce each other. Children put things in their mouth to help them organize perception of taste, feel, size, and shape. When children look at things, they begin to form ideas about space and movement. As they combine these perceptions, they begin to learn the relationships between them. Reading and writing problems that occur when the child is of school age may be caused by faulty or incomplete learning at this stage of development.

At first, children can only name an object, even though they may see it doing many different things. They say "Mommy" or "Car" no matter what the person or the object may be doing. Next they begin to add the idea of movement: "Mommy comes in," or "Daddy drives the car." Later, they add "why" ideas with sentences like "Mommy comes in because I called her," or "Daddy makes the car go to take us to Grandma's house."

In spite of the fact that there is a great deal of learning going on, wise parents learn not to take anything for granted and not to expect too much from young children. Ginny started crying unhappily at the door to her house after being told the family was going to move. When asked what was wrong she said, "The moving man is coming and he's going to take all my things away."

It is important to provide as many opportunities as possible for youngsters to use all of their senses to understand and interpret their experiences. Children learn quite a large number of ideas and actions as a result of observing and emulating the manner in which other children and adults react to their environment. It is not unusual to find a child who is terribly afraid of dogs simply because his mother or older sister does not like them; he may not even have had any direct or frightening experience with them himself. On the other hand, parents sometimes cannot understand a child's fear of dogs when they themselves are not afraid. Careful observation of other neighborhood children and *their* fear of animals will often show that the fear has been learned from them.

"I Thought It Was So Big." (Images and Memories)

Things that have happened in the past are usually referred to as memories. It is obvious that almost all of our ability to evaluate current situations is based upon our memory of past experiences. If a new problem occurs, we usually attempt to select from our past experiences elements that will help us decide how to react to a present situation.

Both children and adults have faulty memories. We sometimes think that things have really happened when we have only imagined them. We also recall past events as we think they have happened; but our memories are colored by our emotions. In one sense, though, these memories are as real as events that are happening at this moment. "I remember," Jimmy says, "the magician sawed the man in half and took a million rabbits out of his hat and disappeared a whole lot of things." There is no doubt in Jimmy's mind that these things actually happened.

Some psychologists continue to debate whether or not we actually retain memories as pictures and, if we do, how they influence the way we think. However, most of them agree that while a small amount of remembering is done without imagery, the largest portion does utilize this form of recall. But, in some children's thinking, other forms of remembering appear to be as important as imagery. For example, the look-say method of teaching children how to read has been only partially effective; all indications point to the fact that teachers should develop techniques that include hearing, touch, and movement as well as seeing.

It is difficult to separate memories (or remembering) from thinking through or acting upon a present problem. Probably the best way to understand how memories influence behavior is to consider them part of a continuum in which the mind retrieves and feeds back information as it relates to a particular problem or course of action. Since the number of experiences related to a particular concept increases with the age of the child, his response pattern becomes more complicated. During the first year, children recall early experiences, but they usually need a real object to help them remember. During the next phase, they may remember things without being stimulated. At first, children remember only people and things; later they remember entire situations and relationships. As they grow older, they remember events for longer periods of time. A concept of time is difficult for children to handle and is usually confused and uncoordinated until the child is five or six. While children recall emotional experiences related to both pain and pleasure, pleasurable experiences dominate their memory by a ratio of more than two to one.

"I Like to Hear the Flutes." (Reactions to Aesthetic Activities)

Children enjoy pictures of things they can understand, and they find rhythmic music pleasurable at as early as eighteen months of age. They like to reproduce musical sounds, sing simple songs, and dance to simple rhythm. Parents who really enjoy the arts will convey their own pleasure to their children. It is usually a mistake to make a great fuss over a piece of music or a work of art; children emulate what you feel and do rather than what you say. When music and art are part of the home, most children will develop a sense of appreciation.

"Look, Mommy. I Built a Bridge." (Problem Solving)

Does a youngster really reason and has he the ability to solve problems during the preschool and early school years? The answer is a resounding Yes. When a child (1) is faced with a task that he understands, (2) sees it as a problem, (3) does not have a quick, easy solution, and (4), tries ideas and finds solutions—then he is engaging in problem-solving activity. This occurs in some children before they are three years old.

In problem solving, as we have previously indicated, there should be a direction and a goal to the child's thinking. If, however, the child does not understand the problem, it becomes more of a puzzle and he will use a random trial-and-error method in attempting to solve it.

In water play, three-year-old Jill fills a large pitcher with water and pours it into a small plastic glass. The glass is filled but Jill continues pouring all of the water out of the pitcher. The result is a glass full of water, a soaked table-cloth, and a wet floor, yet she continues to fill and empty the pitcher several times. Jill does not understand that all the water in the large pitcher will not fit into the small glass, nor does she see the wet tablecloth and floor as a problem. If the child does not recognize a situation as a problem, he will certainly not be motivated to solve it. While children frequently use random trial-and-error methods to solve problems (and sometimes do not try to solve the problems at all), there is a considerable amount of problem solving going on at an early age.

Jed and his nursery school teacher had watched the water running down the street during a spring thaw. They had talked about the sewer and the pipes under the ground and water being carried to the river through the big pipes. After a period of silence, Jed placed his index finger on his forehead and said, "Mmm. Let me think a minute. I think the water comes to the beach from the river."

Problem solving is considerably more complex than the simple association of ideas. A child is usually driven toward trying to solve a problem by strong internal or external motivating forces. Problems usually require immediate responses or solutions; concepts are built up over a long period of time.

Children first develop the ability to solve very specific concrete problems related to immediate situations; their reasoning ability is limited to concrete areas in which they are personally involved. Five-year-old Donald was building a bridge for his toy train, using large nursery school blocks. He stood the tall blocks on end to make one wall, then made another wall opposite the first; to make the roof he placed blocks across the top from one wall to another. The blocks immediately toppled over because there was nothing to hold them up. He used the same method several times, but with no greater success. He surveyed the situation, then left the room and returned with a large piece of corrugated cardboard, which he placed across the walls to form the roof. The cardboard solved the problem, and the project was successful.

Four-year-old Paul walks to the store, asks for one quart of milk, hands the man a quarter, and then walks out with the container cradled safely in his arms. When he returns home, his father's smile tells him that he has done well. This positive feeling then acts to reinforce the behavior. The child has performed an independent act, and Father has made him feel that it was appreciated and desirable.

It is difficult to invent situations that are problems to children. Something that is a problem to an adult may be a puzzle to a child because the child does not completely understand it. When there is a lack of experience or motivation, children have no real desire to solve a problem; they may appear to have failed when in fact they have not even tried. At first, children think only about concrete ideas, but gradually they begin to solve abstract problems by using verbal reasoning. The final phase of learning to think involves children's ability to answer questions in a logical and reasonable fashion.

We need to be careful when we evaluate the success of children's problem-solving activities. Even though a problem may appear only partially or inadequately solved by our standards, we must determine whether the child himself feels that it has been solved. Jane put one block on top of another to reach up to the shelf for her picture book. Since the blocks were quite rocky she had to hold on tightly, but she got her book. A rocky solution, which we may have questioned or discarded, was quite adequate for her. The fact that there was problem-solving behavior going on is the most important element, and we must encourage it. An important part of our vocabulary should include phrases such as, "Try it. Go ahead, don't be afraid. I'll help if you need it. Try it yourself."

The most simple problem solving utilizes the same thinking processes that are used for solving involved problems. Unfortunately, too many parents put heavy emphasis on the *end result,* rather than the *process* itself, and children come away with the mistaken impression that the product is more important than the process. Six-year-old Babs wanted to make Daddy a birthday card and set about the task happily. First she cut the paper (not quite straight); then with loving care she pasted on a picture of a car for Daddy; then she scribbled a message and her name. She ran to Mother, exclaiming, "See, I have a birthday card for Daddy." Mother's frowning reaction told Babs her card was not acceptable. She had learned a lesson. The end product was more important than her attempt to solve her problem. Next time, perhaps, she would not try to solve her problem at all, for fear of coming up with an unacceptable solution, or she might try for a perfect product by buying the card in the store. There was no reward for the process.

"I Like the Cartoons Better." (Critical Evaluation)

During their early years, children do not base evaluations upon logic but upon emotional reactions and associated experiences. Sometimes their evaluations are based on incorrect interpretations of actions or words. "I don't like my teacher," Randy announced as he came home from nursery school.

"Is that so?" asked Mother.

"She lied to me. She said to me, 'You sit here for the present'—and she never brought me any."

As the child grows older, it is all too easy for parents

simply to permit him to make an evaluation, and not ask him how he arrived at his conclusions. This lack of help is due in part to the fact that many adults are often unaware of the reasons for their own actions and seldom think through the reasons for their own conclusions. We should be attempting to help the child learn *how* to judge situations and evaluate them critically.

In helping a child to learn evaluation, be careful how you use the word *why*. When you ask a child, "Why do you say that?" or "Why did you do that?" you appear to be questioning his ability, and his reaction may be to defend his actions rather than analyze them.

"What Is a Witch's Stand?" (Understanding of Language)

"Can you tell me a story about beans?" asked the kindergarten teacher.

"I like bean soup," responds Helen.

"I grew beans in my garden," says George.

"I know one," pipes up James. "We are all human beans."

Children's ability to use language runs parallel with their ability to handle abstract ideas. During the prelanguage development period, and during the early period of speech development, there may be a considerable amount of thinking going on; but, obviously, the addition of language speeds up the process and enables thinking to occur in more abstract areas. It is generally agreed by all those who work with young children that language is an extremely important, if not essential, element in developing the ability to think.

Spoken language is developed gradually, going from words to sentences to more complex ideas. Words are used in thousands of different ways during the early years. One realizes the importance of speech and hearing when one looks at a child who has been deaf from birth. By the age of three or four, because he has not heard spoken language (and therefore has not learned to speak), this child is so far behind in concept formation that it is extremely difficult to make up for the experiences he has missed. It is essential for a deaf child to start his educational program during the first few months of his life.

During the early use of language, young children tend to describe what words mean, rather than defining them as older children and adults do. "Beds are to sleep in," "The straw is to drink," "Kites are to fly," and "Lips are to kiss," are illustrative of how children describe words.

Children find it almost impossible to master every one of the tremendous number of words that they hear, and they are sometimes confused by the fact that the same word symbols and objects mean many different things in different situations. Frequently, they misunderstand and mispronounce words they do not know. Sometimes they "pledge a legents" (what's a legents?) to the flag and "to the republic for witch's stand" (what's a witch's stand?).

Four-year-old Mark is playing with some clay. "Mother, help me make a boat!" he asks. Mother makes a clay tugboat for him to copy. But Mark is thinking of a sailboat like the one in the bottle he has in his room. The experience ends in tears because of the confusion over the specific meaning of "boat."

Johnny wants his mother to take him to nursery school. His mother explains that Ann's mother, Jimmy's mother, and she would take turns driving the three children to school in a car pool. The next morning Johnny asks for his swim suit. Mother laughs and asks why. Johnny says, "You said we were going in a pool."

Children often find pleasure in playing with words and will sometimes deliberately attach funny meanings to them. Word games are enjoyable and help children learn new words.

"I Don't Like You, I Love You." (Emotions)

Why are children in the same family so often different? In addition to differences in heredity, no two children live in exactly the same environment, nor do they have exactly the same experiences. Even identical twins have different environments and experiences from the moment they are born. Obviously one child must be born before the other; they sleep in different parts of the room; one may cry because the other gets fed first. Since environments are not the same for twins, they are certainly different for all other children. Some children live in the country, some in the city. Some parents are strict, others more easygoing.

We must expect certain amounts of emotional difficulties to develop in children, since we obviously cannot create the perfect environment—and in all probability wouldn't want to. At this point, researchers in the area of children's emotions still disagree as to which emotions are inborn and which are learned. In addition, we are not certain what conditions cause which learned emotions. There are obviously many varieties of emotional behavior in children; it depends upon the nature of their inherited and learned traits, and upon the relationship of these traits to one another.

It is difficult for parents to be objective about the emotional behavior of their own children. They tend either to overlook or to look too closely at their children's behavior, perhaps because they are so close to the children. Without being conscious of it, we probably function as if our children were an extension of ourselves. Sometimes, parents will refuse to see that their child is difficult, in spite of all the attempts others make to show them the truth. At the other extreme, some mothers will bring a child to the psychiatrist if he as much as cries when his toy is broken. Since all children will have some emotional difficulties, parents must be prepared to cope with them so that they can help the child overcome them. Professional help should be sought when difficult behavior, such as general unhappiness, illness without physical basis, lack of friends, or open hostility, occurs for a considerable length of time.

Until recently, researchers attempted to determine

which parts of children's thinking were emotionally based and which had been thought through, by separating aspects of the children's behavior. It is generally agreed today that emotional components are an integral part of all the thinking processes and that separation is virtually impossible.

Because the ability to weigh evidence objectively and the experience to support such consideration does not come until later, emotions play a predominant part in the thinking of very young children. For instance, James refuses to stay over at his friend's house—in spite of the fact that he is enjoying himself—because his mother is going home and he is afraid she will not come back to get him.

As with other elements that affect thinking, the role of emotions changes with the experiences of the child. At first, young children's behavior is unrepressed. Soon, however, uninhibited emotions decrease and emotional patterns develop. Jane soon learned that it was not proper to roll in the mud as was her natural inclination. She also quit pulling up her dress to show off her pretty panties.

To look at another aspect of the development of emotions as they relate to thinking, the emotions and attitudes of children often determine what they think about. Emotions govern a child's reactions to new experiences and play an important role in determining his attitudes and values. A child's choice of games, the types of pictures he draws, or his reaction to a story is quite frequently determined by his emotions rather than by an objective thinking process. In many situations, emotions can cause a negative reaction to a new situation, and fear may inhibit a child's willingness to attempt new experiences. Little Sally would not go to a movie because of her fear of the dark. Jane looked out the front windows and would not leave her house when she saw dogs roaming the street. Billy refused ice cream because his mother had warned him about getting his clothes dirty. But Dora jumped into water over her head because she was confident that her father would catch her.

A child's emotional reaction can help him to think on a

very high level; emotions help drive a child to be constantly curious and to think creatively. The critical factor is whether the emotions inhibit thinking or enhance it. Do they muddle the child's thinking, or do they sharpen his perceptions so that he thinks more clearly? The child needs to have emotional security to feel free to act in a creative manner.

Many different emotions appear to influence a child's reaction to a situation. As parents, we are sometimes faced with the problem of deciding how much is too much. When does excitement (which at first appears to improve thinking) become too great and thus inhibit the thought process? When is a problem too difficult? When have we given too much information?

When a child is presented with a problem situation and does not know how to solve it immediately, he is frustrated and perhaps a little disorganized. Six-year-old Kevin was very excited about building a bird house. As he started to try to nail the pieces together, he saw that they did not fit, and frustration set in. He became very irritated and difficult to talk to. The project was too difficult for him and he finally gave up. In some instances, minor frustration is positive and motivates the child to try to work it out; in others, it is overwhelming and the child stops trying entirely. Most parents worry about the point of overwhelming frustration, the point at which they think the child will give up and refuse to participate. As long as the parents do not push—that is, they let the child make his own way—he will usually be safe. If there is any tendency here, it is for parents to move in too soon. On the other hand, though, frustration can lead to anger and resentment, and these reactions may inhibit any further effort to solve the problem. Since children vary in their ability to handle frustration, and since this ability may change from situation to situation, parents can determine the danger point only by careful observation.

Mother bought Johnny a new toy that had to be assembled. Though Johnny literally tore the carton off in his eagerness to put the toy together, the process did not go well.

He began to be frustrated. Mother could have moved in at this point but, knowing that Johnny was not at the point of surrender, decided to hold off. Johnny left the toy for a few minutes but soon came back and asked her to read the directions. When he finally put the toy together (not absolutely correctly) his feelings of success and pride were much greater than if his mother had interceded. It was a wonderful learning experience. (By the way, it would not have done him any harm if he had asked for help and then declined it, or if he had waited until the next day to try again.)

Although small amounts of emotion appear to encourage individuals to make a greater effort, there is considerable evidence that many children cannot work out a problem when the situation is too highly charged emotionally. We have all felt unable to respond adequately to test questions because of fear and anxiety. Giving some children an examination when they are in a highly excitable state only tests how they react to the testing situation—not necessarily how many of the answers they know.

"I Just Don't Like That." (Attitudes)

"I don't think I'm going to like them. I don't like blue things." "I won't have a good time." "I'll be scared." "The noise will frighten me." "If you like it, so will I." What builds up these preconceived notions and attitudes? An attitude is essentially a learned readiness to react to a situation in a certain way. An attitude exerts an influence upon an individual's response to all the objects and situations related to that attitude.

Even preschool and primary school children have a number of well-developed attitudes and appear to be prejudiced, rigid, and influenced by stereotypes. These attitudes, however, are not deeply ingrained, and can be changed very quickly when children have new experiences related to what they already know. However, if these early attitudes are not exposed, discussed, and evaluated objectively, children may tend to return to them as they grow into adulthood.

There are several major methods by which children learn attitudes. *Most frequently, they emulate the attitudes of their parents and others in their environment.* Prejudiced parents often raise prejudiced children. Without any conscious knowledge of what they are learning, children begin to share their parents' ideas about race, religion, labor unions, politics, and neighbors. "Germans are no good. My daddy said so," begins the five-year-old as he teases another child. Young children simply repeat statements without attempting to support or justify them. Older children often break away from the prejudices of their parents and rebel against them.

Attitudes toward animals are often acquired from other children. A child in the neighborhood may be terrified by animals and scream when one comes near. Other young children on the block soon learn this behavior pattern and also start to scream when an animal comes near. Children seem to learn negative responses much more rapidly than they do positive responses.

In some cases, children gain a negative attitude because of some particularly shocking experience. For example, they may have been badly frightened during a storm and are now afraid of all storms. A pleasurable experience usually creates a positive attitude; when children have enjoyed food of a particular color they often continue to like foods of the same color. Four-year-old Tom tells his friends about his latest visit to the doctor. He ends his part of the story with, "My doctor is nice."

"Do you *like* your doctor?" Kay asks, puzzled.

"Yes, he's nice."

"Does he give you shots?"

"Yes."

"Do they hurt?"

"Yes!"

"And you *still* like him?" Kay is even more puzzled.

"Sure. He talks nice to me and he shows me things." Somehow, although each child had a similar experience, Tom developed a positive attitude and Kay a negative one.

Children may act one way in one setting and differently

in another, depending upon their attitudes toward the experience, and upon what is expected of them. An excellent example of the importance of expectancy in influencing behavior occurs in schools for the blind. Too often, blind children are protected and pampered at home whereas in school they are expected to act independently. What are the consequences? At home they cannot do anything without help, while at school they function in a much more independent fashion, running around, eating by themselves, and so on.

New attitudes form during the child's first experiences, so it is important for parents to plan new experiences very carefully. Too often, a child will form an attitude on the basis of only one piece of information, simply because he lacks other information with which to compare it. New ideas, new situations, new friends, and new groups must be introduced in a positive manner that will encourage the child to regard them as pleasant or rewarding experiences. Unfortunately, many adults unthinkingly use expressions that are derogatory to certain groups—"cheap Scots," "Jew him down," "shanty Irish." Children hear these expressions and form prejudiced attitudes. By the time a child enters school, he has a well-developed set of surface attitudes.

If a child finds that doing new things is usually pleasurable, he will tend to have positive attitudes toward new ideas and experiences and will be willing to try whatever the parent or teacher suggests. Rita sits down at the table at nursery school announcing that she doesn't like that color juice. The teacher says, "Rita, you don't have to like it but take a taste anyway." Rita tastes it and discovers it's not like the juice she had before. She drinks two glasses. Although she had a negative attitude toward this color of juice, she felt secure enough to participate in a new experience. Unfortunately, the opposite reaction is also common. We find children refusing to try new things, to accept new ideas, or to participate in new experiences because of earlier frustration or adult displeasure.

Concepts are founded upon information, while attitudes are based more upon emotional experiences. As attitudes become more permanent, they may be called values. *When thinking, imagination, curiosity, and discovery are encouraged within the home, the child grows up holding these as positive values.*

"I Didn't Think About It." (Habits)

"Why do you count on your fingers?" Mother asks.

"I don't know, I always counted that way," responds little Julia. Certain habits may have a great deal of bearing on whether or not children think effectively. A habit is an acquired act that becomes a fixed response to a particular situation. Habits become relatively unconscious—almost automatic—responses and tend to result in stereotyped thinking and behavior. When children learn to solve problems utilizing only one specific method they have difficulty working out solutions to problems that require a flexible approach.

"Buttons Are to Push." (Concepts)

Proudly holding up his drawing, which was covered entirely with different size circles, six-year-old Paul signaled that he had finished. Pulling the paper out of his hand, his first grade teacher announced in a loud voice, "What a mess, Paul. Can't you do something neat and nice instead of just messing up your paper?" Paul was crushed. Tearfully he asked to show his drawing to his former teacher in kindergarten. Permission granted, Paul rushed out and excitedly entered the kindergarten room. The teacher looked up, somewhat amazed at his precipitous arrival. "What have we here?" she asked.

"I wanted to show you my drawing. It took me a long time. I just finished it." The teacher looked down at the paper, filled with carefully drawn circles of all sizes. "What a nice drawing," she said. "Tell me about it."

"They're buttons," Paul stated with emphasis. "All

kinds of buttons. These are for a rocket, this one rings a bell, this one blows a siren, this one. . . . You know, buttons are to push."

A concept is a generalized notion; it includes a wide variety of ideas related to a central idea. Those of us who work with children are not quite sure exactly how they form their concepts. We are certain, however, that concept formation starts at quite an early age. The earliest steps probably involve the child's sensory impressions of the world and the meanings that he attaches to them. Without any direct instruction, children appear to learn a great deal about the elements in their environment. They attach a certain image (Mother) to comfort. A particular smell means food, and the sound of a car means Father is coming home. New information is constantly added to the concepts that they are forming, and the concepts themselves are in constant change. Children soon learn where things are in the house and how to get from one place to another. As they have more experiences, they fit them in with the concepts they are forming, or they begin building new ones.

Young children build up concepts when they begin to see relationships between things and learn to discriminate between them. They form concepts by generalizing from the information they have. At first, they begin to generalize from simple abstractions. For instance, they soon learn that "door" refers to many different sizes and kinds of doors in many different places. Later they attach characteristics to concrete objects, such as *noisy* to pots and *soft* to pillows.

Investigators report that *breadth of experience helps children in concept formation much more than a specific intense type of training*. Thus, it is more important for children to have a variety of experiences than to have the same experience frequently or in depth.

Children have difficulty with words that are related to abstract concepts. At dinner one evening, three-year-old Susie informed her family that her nursery school teacher was God. Susie's mother tried to explain that this was not so.

In a determined manner Susie retorted, "Yes, she is too God. She brings us our juice, and then we sit down at the table and say, 'Thank you God for this juice.' "

In developing his concepts, the child learns about different properties of things. Things may move, like cars, or stand still, like the house he lives in. They may be heavy, like the piano, or light, like a piece of paper or his pencil. Some things can be counted, like his crayons; some things come in bunches, like candies in a bag. Children develop a concept of events and how they relate to each other. Most children have learned hundreds of concepts by the age of four.

We can see, therefore, that from very early infancy the young child has been learning to generalize and discriminate between ideas, to gain from his experience, and to sift out the important elements of his environment. A baby seems to know the meaning of approaching footsteps and begins to gurgle and jump when he hears them. He has attached the sound to feeding or to the comfort of his mother's presence. He is connecting two ideas. Sometimes, an infant may learn at an early age to discriminate by color between foods he likes and those he dislikes. He learns the consequences of laughing, crying, and pulling, and thus begins to manipulate his environment. As new concepts are learned, the child becomes more capable of handling his environment, more able to deal with problems as they occur, and more adept at solving situations as they confront him.

If we did not have concepts within which to fit our experiences and integrate individual facts, we would be unable to react thoughtfully to particular situations because we would have to go through all the facts we possessed and select out those that were pertinent. Without concepts, it would be almost impossible to cope with our environment.

Hopefully, concepts themselves never become complete. Children and adults should always be willing to add information to the concepts they hold. Individuals with a closed system of concepts find it extremely difficult to understand and accept new ideas, to react to new surroundings objectively, and to permit new ideas to change the way they function.

Concepts are formed from perceptions, attitudes, images, memories, and imagination. They utilize language and other means of communication in their formation. There are wide differences among children of the same age in the number and completeness of the concepts they hold. The greater the number and variety of experiences, the broader and more accurate are the formation and expansion of concepts.

IMAGINATION AND
DIRECTIONAL THINKING

We have used and will continue to use the terms *curiosity, imagination, problem solving, critical evaluation,* and *creativity* so frequently that it appears worthwhile to take a deeper look into what they mean, and to discuss what we know about them.

IS CURIOSITY EVER IDLE?

After Thorstein Veblen, the economist, ridiculed "idle" curiosity, he was taken to task by the historian James H. Robinson, who said, "Curiosity is idle only to those who fail to realize that it may be a very rare and indispensable thing. . . . Idle curiosity leads to creative thoughts."

Curiosity is very difficult to analyze or measure—or even define. We have learned that curiosity must be nurtured and treated with loving care. It is relatively easy to arouse but almost impossible to re-create once it has been snuffed out. It has been described as a "tendency toward investigation" or as "being interested in searching and in learning new things." It is all that and more. For children, curiosity may be observed as a kind of probing and wandering, an undirected adventure into uncharted areas.

"Jill, where are you, Jill?" cries Mother, searching for her three-year-old.

"Here I am, Mommy," comes a tiny, muffled voice from somewhere in the bedroom.

Hurrying in, Mother looks around and calls, "Where, Jill?"

"Here I am, in the closet." Mother opens the door and there is Jill, almost hidden under a pile of clothes and shoes, smiling with obvious enjoyment. "I just wanted to see what was in here," she says innocently, as Mother pulls her out. Parents remember a great many frightening experiences —the thumb caught in the faucet, the hand in the milk bottle— and other impossible situations that children get themselves into because of their wonderfully uncontrollable curiosity.

There Was a Young Maid Who Said "Why"

There was a young maid who said "Why
Can't I look in my ear with my eye?
If I give my mind to it,
I'm sure I can do it,
You never know till you try."

Edward Lear

Parents who really care about their children's safety

must protect them by keeping dangerous things out of their reach. Restraining children by prohibiting them from going into certain places and doing certain things is more for the convenience of the parents than for the good of the child. Indeed, telling a child not to do something or not to go to a certain place is frequently an open invitation to a young child's curiosity.

While curiosity may be fatal to cats, the lack of curiosity would undoubtedly be fatal to man. It has been curiosity and our willingness to try out new ideas that has advanced us to our present stage of development. Things that are new don't just happen; they are the result of someone's imagination. Curiosity and the question Why? go together. This curiosity is part of "self-starting" and, with help, can result in a habitually interested and curious response to life and its experiences.

Curiosity is the basis of directional thinking: without the question Why? there would be little experimentation and problem solving. There can be no problem solving without a feeling that a problem exists. Without the desire to understand and to improve the world around us, there would be little critical evaluation, and without the motivation to try new ideas or do things in a new way, there would be little creative endeavor.

Curiosity is the very essence of effective or directional thinking. The curious child becomes the inquiring adult. The adult who lost his curiosity while he was growing up will be the type of person who says, "That's the way things are," "Can't fight City Hall," or "What can I do about it?" At first, parents have the responsibility of discovering methods to sustain and promote curiosity in ways that are meaningful to the child. Later, teachers can help. Every child possesses the quality of curiosity. It is up to us to help him retain it, broaden it, use it, and build upon it.

While man has created machines that will perform many jobs more rapidly than human beings, and has even invented machines that appear to apply reason to problems, no one has been able to come up with a machine that possesses imagination. We are still dependent upon man's imagination for the continued survival of our world.

Imagination includes a kind of mental picture—that is, the ability to retain mental images of things and ideas and to form relationships between them and concepts not yet in sight.

Those who use their imagination are continuously imagining alternative ways of seeing things or solving problems. Imagination has a close relationship to creativity, and children are frequently both imaginative and creative when they play.

Robert comes running up to his father with a serious expression on his face. "I've got a problem, Dad."

"Oh, how can I help?" Dad responds.

"Well," explains Robert, "I've been a giant all morning, walking around in the mountains and woods and I'm so big and the ground is so rough that I've just about worn out my shoes. Now where am I going to get another pair of shoes?"

"Now that's a problem," Dad agrees. "What ideas have you tried?"

"Well, I can't go to a regular small-man shoemaker. He would have to use up all his leather, and I'm a good giant so I wouldn't want to do that. I've thought of making my own shoes but I'm not sure I know how and, besides, I don't know where to get the leather anyhow. I can't figure out what to do."

"Got any other ideas?" asks Dad.

"Nope," replies Robert, pondering his problem.

"Where did you get the first pair of shoes?" asks Dad.

"Why, in the giant town where I came from. I get it, Dad, I'll go back there and find the giant shoemaker and get him to make me a pair. Thanks, Dad, that was a tough problem." Robert trudges off with a sigh of relief.

We can study children's imagination by observing their

play, how they dramatize, how they construct things, and how they use language. Imagination represents freedom for the mind. Children dream, make up fanciful characters and stories, and make their wishes come true by using their imagination.

Four-year-old Stan has been asking his parents for a bicycle for several weeks. His father has put him off, saying he didn't have any money now. One morning at the breakfast table Stan looks quite sad. "What's the matter?" his mother asks, noticing this unusual behavior.

"Well," Stan replied, "last night I dreamed I had a new bicycle, and I tried and tried to take it out of my dream but I couldn't. I'm going to try again tonight."

In their imagination, children find it easy to solve their problems. They use imagination in a number of ways. Sometimes they plan activities by imagining what would happen if they did them. They attach imaginary meaning to drawings, music, and dancing, or they simply use their imagination to enjoy themselves in play.

The Perfect Reaction

As I was sitting in my chair
I knew the bottom wasn't there
Nor the legs nor back, but I just sat
Ignoring little things like that.

Hughes Mearns

Some children have imaginary companions, and they take great delight in inventing names and characteristics for these playmates. In many cases, the imaginary friends fill a specific need. Perhaps the child does not have enough real-life friends to play with, or he may be reacting to a difficult situation at home (rivalry with a sibling, for example, or a problem with Mother or Father). Parents should not be concerned about a child's friendship with an imaginary person unless it is carried to the extreme where the child always plays only with imaginary friends and does not make any other friends, or if the friendship continues after the child starts to go to school.

As children grow older, many of them lose their ability to use their imagination. The problems they face and have to solve become more related to the real world. Situations confronting them at home and at school are usually not conducive to an imaginative approach, because the solutions they invent must now face the test of reality.

DIRECTIONAL THINKING

Problem Solving

There are a number of approaches or steps to problem solving.

The first of these steps is an awareness that a problem exists and a desire to solve it. Second, there must be a clear understanding of the problem. Third, there is usually a gathering of information or a determination of the essential elements of the problem. Fourth, there is a trying or testing of formulated ideas or hypotheses and a judging of their effectiveness. Finally, the problem solver must decide upon a solution or conclusion or go back to step two to re-examine the problem. Although these steps apply in general to almost all problems, the process may vary with the type and difficulty of a particular problem.

The all-important first step in problem solving is recognizing that a problem exists. If a child does not see or understand that there is a problem, he does not seek a solution. Once the child becomes aware of a problem, he must feel that he can take action to solve it. If he thinks he cannot do anything about it, it does him no good to see a situation as a problem.

When a child is very young, problems are usually recognized only if they are real and he can see them. He can think about how to get over a puddle of water or how to build a roof on a house made of blocks. The solutions are usually trial and error and also tend to be of a concrete nature. Older children develop the ability to deal with abstract ideas. They may try some solutions by thinking rather than by doing. For instance, they may mentally measure a piece of wood to see if it is suitable for building a house. As the ability to deal with concepts and relationships develops, children soon learn to see cause-and-effect relationships, and can often test a solution by mental reasoning.

In too many instances, parents and teachers require children to solve problems without determining whether or not the child understands the problem and has the information required to solve it. Asking a child to find out all he can about one of the fifty states may appear to a teacher to be a meaningful problem, but the child who has little concept of the difference between a city and a state, and does not know where the state is located, is faced not with a problem but with an exercise in memory. When a child is presented with such a situation, it becomes a problem of how to satisfy the teacher rather than one of finding out about a state. Children quickly learn that in school it is important to satisfy the teacher and this becomes the motivation for their behavior.

When children do not understand problems or when they have too little information, they attempt to arrive at solutions by gross trial-and-error behavior rather than through the logical sequence of thought, plan of action, and application. Since children differ in learning rates, what may be a real problem to one child may generate no interest in another.

A child's motivation and his attitudes toward problem solving are important factors. While some children see problem solving as an adventure, others seek solutions with a great deal of trepidation. When children feel that their attempts to solve problems are appreciated and are secure in the knowledge that help is available, they are more likely to develop positive, healthy attitudes toward problem solving.

Critical Evaluation or Thinking

The terms *"critical* evaluation'' and *"critical* thinking'' should not be interpreted as meaning ''negative,'' for criticism can be both positive and negative. Although it is impossible to separate critical evaluation entirely from its partners, problem solving and creative thinking, it still has enough substance to be considered by itself.

David Russell suggests that there are four conditions involved in critical evaluation. Compare with problem solving:

(1) a general knowledge of the material

(2) questioning of ideas before accepting them

(3) application of some logical method of analysis

(4) acting upon one's judgment

There are many acts of critical evaluation that are not based upon the above principles and that often cause a great deal of confusion and mistrust. Too often, individuals and groups make judgments and form conclusions without the necessary knowledge upon which to base them. Children are usually taught, both directly and indirectly, to accept the statements of adults, books, newspapers, radio, and television. Believe it or not, even well-known encyclopedias sometimes give erroneous information. While it would be unwise to teach children to question every written word and every adult utterance, it is important to encourage the child to take a critical attitude toward information that he is considering using to form an opinion or solve a problem.

Children need our assistance to help them develop the habit of suspending judgment since, in general, their environment does not present material in such a way that children have an opportunity to evaluate it. Too often, children are taught to make conclusions on the basis of emotion or superstition.

What About Creativity?

Creativity is a capacity possessed to some extent by all children, rather than a specific ability that is given to only a few. Since many people do not understand this ability, it has acquired a somewhat mystical aura—as something that comes forth without any assistance at opportune moments. More and more today, it is becoming accepted that creative ability can be trained and improved by special techniques, and that, with careful research, we will be able to discover these techniques. Researchers also assume that some aspects of creativity can be measured by the use of tests and other evaluative instruments.

Researchers have indicated, however, that there is no more complicated characteristic than creativity. They suggest that creativity depends upon a large number of individual actions that apparently combine in a variety of ways to make up the single act we call "creativity." Included are originality, flexibility, imagination, ideational fluency, inquisitiveness, productivity, visualization, judgment, ingenuity, sensitivity to problems, associational fluency, powers of synthesis, analysis, redefinition, and others.

John Ciardi, writing in the *Saturday Review* (December 15, 1956), gave a simple definition that covers most creative acts and is worth remembering: "Creativity is the imaginatively gifted recombination of known elements into something new."

The study of creativity has long been neglected in the United States, and it is only recently that a nationwide emphasis on the study of its roots, its nature and nurture, and its consequences has begun.

J. P. Guilford, in the *American Psychologist* (April, 1959), discussed two kinds of thinking and their relationship to creative behavior. He refers to them as *divergent thinking* and *convergent thinking*. Divergent thinking is the type that most characterizes creative thinking. It is speculative, and takes off from information already possessed. Convergent thinking is more conservative in character; it uses information to find an existing answer. Schools usually present questions that call for convergent thinking—single correct answers. Too seldom are children given questions that encourage them to use their own ideas for answers or that encourage a number of possible answers. Compare these two questions that a teacher may ask after the children have read a story: "What did the pilot do when the plane reached the airport?" and "Why do you think the pilot landed at this airport?" The first demands a single answer provided in the book (convergent thinking). The second asks the children to think of many possible answers (divergent thinking).

Studies of creativity show that a comparatively large percentage of creative children do not score high on conventional intelligence tests. Indeed, intelligence tests overlook many of the children with the highest creative ability. E. Paul Torrance, who has done imaginative work on creativity in children, writes in his book *Guiding Creative Talent* that creative ability increases through the third grade, where it drops. Then it goes up again through the seventh grade, where it again drops, this time rather sharply. One explanation for the decrease in creativity is that school conditions cause the child to conform.

There is a good deal of evidence that teachers prefer students with high IQs who conform, rather than highly creative individuals. They often fail to support creative endeavors of their pupils. The conditions that encourage effective or directional thinking are the same conditions that encourage creativity. They include rewards for creative thinking, psychological freedom to think, background skills and experiences, and stimulating situations.

Children soon learn that it is unwise to ask certain questions or to suggest that there may be other alternatives to their teachers' ideas. One junior high school student failed a course in elementary geometry. This was difficult to understand, since her achievement scores showed that she was two years ahead of her class average and had received A's in all her courses, including math. She was questioned closely by her father, who was a professor in college, and by her mother, who was also a teacher, but they were unable to discover why she had failed. Suddenly she started to receive high grades. When her parents asked what had happened to cause the change, she said, "Oh, I found it wasn't a good idea to question the teacher and try out new ways—*all you have to do is what you are told.*"

The creative child has a difficult road to walk and needs all the support he can get. Even without any assistance, many children overcome difficult obstacles and become creative adults. Think how many more would achieve this essential goal with a little help and support from us!

ENCOURAGING CREATIVITY AND EFFECTIVE THINKING

I Can Be a Tiger

I can't go walking
When they say no,
And I can't go riding
Unless they go.
I can't splash puddles
In my shiny new shoes,
But I can be a tiger
Whenever I choose.

I can't eat peanuts,
And I can't eat cake.

I have to go to bed
When they stay awake.
I can't bang windows
And I mustn't tease,
But I can be an elephant
As often as I please.

Mildred Leigh Anderson

We have previously discussed the child's world: how he develops in the various areas which form the bases for curiosity, imagination, and the ability to think effectively. Now we will discuss specific ways that parents can help their children grow into adults who use imagination in solving problems, who critically evaluate their experiences, and who can live creatively.

Most people will agree that in order to think intelligently about a problem one must have some facts upon which to base one's thinking and test one's solutions. It is important to point out, however, that facts are helpful only when we are able to *use* them in a meaningful way. We may study facts all day, but they cannot help us unless we are able to use them. Indeed, when people have too many facts, or place too great a reliance on factual material, their curiosity, imagination, and creativity are sometimes inhibited.

What actually goes on in a child's mind is a mystery to adults, although parents and teachers themselves form the background against which children have their childhood experiences. They provide the atmosphere in which the child experiments and learns. As the child moves from complete dependence toward independence, the parents' role changes, but it still plays an essential part in development and support.

A little boy named Robert showed his growing independence when he described the children singing songs at the birthday party of his three-year-old friend. When asked what they sang he said, "I don't know what the others sang but I sang the Alphabet Song.'"

WHAT PARENTS CAN DO

In general, we are concerned here with encouraging the activities and ideas in a child's environment that may be of positive value in his growth and development. We can help children sustain and develop curiosity, imagination, and creativity by offering them freedom to experiment with their environment and with new ideas, and limiting them only when there is physical danger. This means, for example, letting them play with pots and pans and encouraging them to make their own toys.

"Tell me more about what you want to know." "That's an interesting question." These are the responses that encourage children to learn through asking questions, for they indicate an approving parental attitude.

"That's a great idea. Do you have any more?" "How would we work out that idea?" "Let's try to do that together." These replies show children you place positive value on their ideas. They help children test their ideas themselves.

Children are sensitive to the stimuli that surround them, particularly when these are called to their attention. Parents who comment about pretty smells, who enjoy good cooking, or who react emotionally to beautiful scenery, painting, and art, help children learn to appreciate these aspects of life. The child's education is the sum total of all his experiences. When a child sees the people around him read poetry or listen to music, he is encouraged to investigate these activities for himself.

Young children have little time sense and usually demand immediate rewards and the immediate fulfillment of promises. When parents use terms like "just a minute," "wait a few minutes," "later," or "tomorrow," they are helping their child learn about time.

"Jerry, it's time to come inside," Mother calls.

"But, Mom, I'll be finished in five minutes," Jerry pleads.

"When I say come inside, I mean it. *Come in right now!*" Mother commands with unbending rigidity. We don't advocate permitting children to do as they please nor are we in favor of absolute obedience. Both extremes hurt children and keep them from developing to their full potential. All children quarrel with what you ask them to do from time to time—some more, some less. A child should have some freedom to finish what he is doing if it is at all possible. It just takes a little better planning to change the above dialogue to, "Say, Jerry, you'll have to come inside in ten minutes so finish what you are doing."

"Okay, Mom." Give a little notice. It helps so much. There will probably still be some arguments, but they will occur less frequently and be of less duration.

Certain patterns of parental behavior inhibit curiosity, imagination, and creativity—and thus stifle effective thinking. It is important that we do not force our ideas on children. Children's ideas are important to them and should be important to us. If a parent refuses to consider a child's ideas, then the child will feel that they are not worthwhile and will soon stop offering them.

Some adults manipulate children for their own pleasure or satisfaction. Others pressure them because of their own needs and desires. This includes requiring them to function as little adults rather than children—they must achieve high marks in school, like the things we like, react to situations the way we react. Mistakes are part of learning. We must look at the total process and consider that correcting mistakes is all part of learning. There is nothing wrong with helping a child with his idea—as long as you explain the basis for each action you take and let him contribute as much as he can. He will learn from what you say or do, and then be able to go off on his own.

Perhaps the greatest mistake parents make is that they plan too much of a child's time and routinize his life so that there is little time for free play and just being a child. Eliminate the expression, ''I'm only doing this for your own good.'' Both you and your child will probably feel better if you don't use it.

The Need to Explore

Children are constantly exploring their environment. The baby jabs at the bars of his crib and at the mobile as it floats above him. The crawler is in cabinets and closets, pulling out pots and pans, shoes, and everything else he can find. The toddler pokes his nose into every corner of the house, pulling and pushing anything he can move. The nursery school child carefully examines the environment outside of the house, looks under each bush, and plays with crayons, clay, blocks, and finger paint. The primary school child loves picture books and new places to visit. Freedom to explore and manipulate are important to the curious, developing mind. Some limitations are definitely necessary for the child's protection but, too often, too many restrictions are enforced.

Are you embarrassed by pots and pans on your kitchen floor? Are too many rooms off limits to children in your house? Most parents would like to have one off-limits place; for a man it is usually his shop or office and for a woman it is often the living room. If you don't want children in these places, close them off instead of scolding the children when they enter them. Having a place that's interesting for a child and then forbidding him to go there is like handing him a lollipop and then slapping his hand when he reaches for it.

Count the number of times you say ''Don't'' each day. Try to remember that doing something isn't wrong just because it has not been done before. New things are fun. Before you say ''Don't,'' stop and ask yourself, ''Why not?'' If parents say ''Don't'' too often, it either begins to lose its meaning or *restricts the child to the point where he refuses to try anything*.

Billy came running into the kitchen and reported breathlessly, ''I built a house that was bigger than me, Mom.''

"That's a fib, Billy, and you know it. Why do you say things like that?"

"No, Mom. Honest. I built it taller than me but it fell down." We know that it's important to help children learn to tell the truth but it is sometimes wise to wait until the child is ready to distinguish reality from imagination. At an early age, children have trouble distinguishing imaginative occurrences from real happenings. Rather than crushing their imaginative ability, we need to encourage this talent by telling them imaginative stories and encouraging them to act out their imaginative ideas. After all, imagination is only the ability to make something that is absent become something real. The test of reality comes soon enough. Too often, reality actually inhibits us when we attempt to think or solve problems imaginatively.

Encourage your child's fanciful ideas. He will live a richer, more vibrant life. Permit the freedom of dragons flying around your house, a crowded jungle in the yard, suits of armor under the stairs, or flying saucers circling the playroom.

"Would you like to play a game?" asks Mother of Priscilla, who is four years old.

"Sure, Mommy. Sure I'd like to play a game. What game? What's the game?" Priscilla is considerably interested.

"Well," says Mother, "let's play a game of how many things you can name."

"How do you play it?"

"Let's see," says Mother. "Name as many things as you can think of that fly."

"That's easy. There's birds. And airplanes and leaves, Mommy. Leaves fly too. And snow. That flies. And," she adds, giggling, "and girls skirts fly, don't they, Mommy? They fly too."

"Yes," replies Mommy, quite impressed with her daughter's imagination, "they do fly too."

Too often, we make assumptions about what children want to do and, as a result, force them to follow our own ideas. How often have we seen Father correcting his little boy in the

use of a new toy? When children look at a new toy without
any preconceived idea of how it works and how to play with
it, their imagination sometimes takes over. If they know we
are not going to ridicule their efforts, they obtain a considerable amount of enjoyment from creating new uses and games.
After all, what will these children really have missed if a whole
week goes by before they learn what the manufacturer thought
they ought to do with the toy?

THE VALUE OF QUESTIONS

If we accept the idea that questions are the basis of learning,
then children must feel free to ask questions until they are
satisfied with the answers. "Why do I hear noises?"

"Sounds are carried through the air. They go in your
ears and make a kind of drum vibrate. This sends a message
to your brain and then you have heard the sound."

"Is there a drum in my ears?"

"Well, it's like a drum—some skin is stretched over
some bones."

"Can I see the drum?"

"No, you can't see it in the ear, but perhaps you can
find a picture of it in your encyclopedia if you want to."

"How does sound go through the air?" And on and on
and on.

Parents don't have to answer any really silly questions
like "If the sky were purple, instead of blue, what would happen?" or "Why is up, up?" Nor do parents have to respond
to questions every time a child takes a fancy to ask one. Although children should feel free to ask questions, parents
should also feel free to say, "Will you remember to hold that
question for later? I am eating (or reading or watching TV)
right now." But please try to remember that later does
come.

Children will learn to respect your rights, especially
when you are aware of theirs.

Although each family must determine its own best time for questions, there are some special times during the day and week that are the right times for many people. For mother it may be just after the children arrive home from school and are getting out of their school clothes. For both mother and father it may be right before supper, right after supper, bedtime, or when the family is riding along in the car. Many families have found it worthwhile to reserve a portion of time each day (and it may be as little as fifteen minutes) to answer and ask questions.

Even with planned time, it would be cruel to deny a child's question when you see he is exploding with curiosity. A flexible approach teaches flexibility, which is an important asset to children who are learning to think.

Let's look for a moment at responses to questions. It is probably worthwhile to remind ourselves that children sometimes pop questions without any forethought and without any deep interest. There are a variety of possible responses that an adult can make to a child's question.

Jane, who is riding in the front seat of the family car with her father, says, "Daddy, what's that you keep your foot on when you're driving? Does that make the car go?" Daddy is encouraged by this question. What an observant child, he thinks to himself proudly. And only four years old. I must tell her about these things in terms that she can understand. "That's an accelerator," he says. "When I push it down, it makes the motor go faster and the motor makes the wheels and the car go faster."

"Oh. Make the car go faster," Jane says gleefully, and the conversation is finished. Father feels quite proud of himself because he explained everything so that Jane understands. He even asks, "Jane, do you understand now?" and Jane replies, "Yes, Daddy." Sounds good. Everything appears to have been handled satisfactorily, but Father missed a wonderful opportunity to help Jane learn by using her powers of observation and her ability to reason.

He might have said, "Oh, you noticed that my foot is on that when we drive. What happens when I take my foot off?"—taking his foot off.

"The car slows down," says Jane.

"And when I press it down a little harder, what happens?"

"The car goes faster."

"Right," says Father.

"Oh, this is fun," says Jane. "That pedal must make the car go. Does it make the car go, Daddy?"

"What do you think?" asks Father.

"Yes, yes it does, when you push it down the car goes faster and when you take your foot off, the car slows down and it stops."

"Yes, Jane. This is called a gas pedal, or the big word is accelerator. Can you say that?" Jane is encouraged to ask more questions, and her father encourages her to think them through and take a guess at the answers.

Contrast the two conversations and consider how often a parent responds too quickly to a child's query. But how exciting it must be for a child to learn by thinking through ideas!

Questions are the verbal manifestations of a child's curiosity. *The manner in which adults respond to his questions determines whether a child's curiosity will grow or will slowly be extinguished.*

In addition, the techniques the child learns in finding answers (setting up hypotheses, testing them, drawing conclusions) and the information he gains in the process, both help train him to solve problems and add to his knowledge. Research shows that when children understand information they retain it longer than when they have only memorized it.

"What do *you* think?" is a most important part of a parent's technique for helping his children. It takes a great deal of time and self-discipline to learn to respond with, "What do *you* think?" rather than with "Yes," "No," or a flat statement that cuts off the discussion.

"Can you make smoke with a magnifying glass, Daddy?"

"Yes," replies Daddy, "you can. By holding it in the sun and focusing the rays of the magnifying glass with a piece of paper or something that will burn. Understand?" The conversation is thus terminated. Father has discharged his obligation by giving the answer, but he has missed an opportunity to help his child think through a problem, or for them to discover things together.

While some children—depending upon their level of development—may not have the ability to respond intelligently to "What do you think?" you will be surprised at how observant and willing to try out hypotheses many very young children are. "What do you think?" will bring some interesting and worthwhile responses that may come as a shock to adults because they are likely to be naïve about what the children know. Of course, it would be the height of foolishness to respond to *all* questions with "What do you think?" The response must vary with the type of question asked.

"Daddy, where does our electricity come from?" asks Harold.

"That is an interesting question," replies Dad. "Do you have any ideas?" (This is another way of saying, "What do you think?")

"Nope," Harold responds, with a shrug of his shoulders.

"Do you think it comes from the outside?" Dad persists.

"I dunno, well, yes, I guess it must come from somewhere outside. Those wires attached to our house that come from the pole in the street. Does that have anything to do with it?"

"Now you're on the right track," says Dad approvingly. "Can you figure out [another way of saying, "What do you think?"] where these wires go to in our house?"

"In the basement," Harold retorts.

"Let's go look," suggests Dad and they march down to the basement.

CHILDREN LEARN BY DOING

"Mom," shouts little Billy from outside. "Can I have a piece of rope, Mom?"

"What do you want a piece of rope for?" asks Mom, in the middle of peeling potatoes.

"I want to make a train with the bicycles and wagons," Billy replies.

"No, you can't have any rope," Mom replies, irritated by the interruption. "You'll hurt yourself."

"I promise," Billy pleads. "We won't hurt ourselves, we'll be careful."

"No, no. Don't bother me now. Don't you see I'm busy? Now go play with the wagons and the bicycles *the way they are supposed to be played with.*"

"But, Mom, bikes and wagons are a train," says Billy as he retreats.

"Mom, Mom, look at this pretty rock I found. Isn't it pretty? Look at the colors that run through the rock," Laura shouts excitedly, running into the house holding her precious rock.

"Laura Leona Rossiter, get that filthy rock out of the house. We don't want dirt in here," responds Mother in an annoyed tone.

"But can I save it, Mom? Can I save it and show it to Dad? I want to collect pretty rocks. They're nice and they will make a nice collection," pleads Laura.

"No. Absolutely not. Now take that thing out of here and get rid of it. We don't want to have a messy house, do we?" retorts Mother.

"I guess not," says Laura tearfully, holding her precious stone and losing another bit of her curiosity.

Every time a child makes a request, we should certainly not be expected to drop everything and devote our attention to him, but there are so many times when, with a little bit of effort, we could keep the spark of curiosity alive. Unfortunately, we are all too often unwilling to make the effort. We give money and material things like books and records (which are needed) but rarely do we give enough time. In many cases, we verbalize our desire to help children learn to think, but in practice we do the opposite.

In the midst of having her milk and cookies, Roberta sits up and exclaims, "Mom, I have an idea. I'd like to bake a cake. Can I, Mom?"

"That's a good idea," Mother replies. "Let's see what it would take to bake a cake. Would you like to try a cake mix first and perhaps another time we might start with our things? Do we have a cake mix in the pantry? Will you look?" Roberta dashes to the pantry and is back in a flash with a chocolate cake mix.

"My favorite, Mom. Chocolate!"

"Let's see what it says on the box," Mother says. "Oh. It says it will take forty minutes after we put it in the oven and we have to leave in twenty minutes to pick up your brother. What shall we do?"

"Will we have time when we come back?" asks Roberta.

"I think so. Why don't we talk about the instructions so we can get started as soon as we're back."

"Dad, can we build a scat car?" says seven-year-old Matt. "I saw some beauties the other day."

"That's an interesting idea," says Dad. "Let's see if we can figure out what we would need and how to build one. What do you think we'd need, Matt?"

"A motor, wheels, a steering wheel—those are the big things. We'd also need lots of small things like nuts and bolts and chains. Gee, Dad, that sounds like it would be pretty hard to do."

"You're right, son. It's quite a project—and it's expensive too. Maybe we can find something easier. Let's see . . ."

Not all conversations with children are as clear-cut as

these, but they are samples of some approaches parents can use to give support and positive value to children's ideas.

If it weren't so sad, we would all be amused by the parent or teacher who says, "I want you to think," or "Use your head. Think," as if children could perform like puppets. Commanding a child to think is as ridiculous as commanding him to sing if he hasn't learned how. Most adults think that children can continue to learn by discovery without any assistance, but children can get only so far in utilizing their surroundings by themselves. While we have stated repeatedly that children appear to be naturally curious and imaginative, we must emphasize the point that children can be kept from developing to their full potential by being denied access to new situations. The lack of a stimulating, expanding environment can, and does, inhibit growth in learning ability. As a child is confronted with a new situation, his curiosity encourages exploration and his imagination suggests new relationships. He tries to fit the information he acquires into existing or new concepts. He is learning by discovering new elements in the new experience.

The opposite of this is to just present new information and facts. Unfortunately, teachers are often under pressure to cover a large amount of material, and this forces them to present a great many facts without giving students time to understand and use them.

When children take trips, they are interested in learning more than bits and pieces of information. While at first they may only want to know the names of animals at the zoo, they are soon interested in learning other facts about them— where they live, what they eat, and so forth. It is not enough simply to expose children to experiences; they need help in learning to observe. The excitement that parents show when they observe things carries over to the children and motivates them to be more responsive to their environment. Parents who comment upon what they see and feel, and who ask questions ("What do you think about that?" "How does that make you feel?" "How do you think that works?" "Does that remind you of anything you have seen before?") stimulate their children to think about their surroundings and experiences and to express their feelings about them.

Parents must be careful, however, not to introduce youngsters to new ideas and experiences before they are ready for them. One often finds parents dragging unwilling youngsters off to museums, or forcing them to sit through concerts because they believe that exposing children to these things is important in their growth and development. Although some children are ready for some exposure to these experiences, the careful parent always underplays rather than overplays an interest. Another type of problem may arise when the child *does* evidence interest in some new area and overanxious parents become too involved. Then too often the child loses interest. Five-year-old Stewart expressed an interest in trains. Immediately Dad spent $300 for a model train set and spent several weeks setting it up. When it was all finished, Stewart played with it for about an hour and once every six months thereafter.

When we are forced to do something against our will, we often react by disliking or resenting what we have to do. The best way to extinguish enthusiasm is to force children into activities in which they have no interest or are not mature enough to handle. Parents who drag uninterested youngsters to concerts or museums may extinguish the very interest they wish to foster.

How does the parent determine what a youngster is ready for? This is a difficult question because the answer differs with each youngster and each situation, but if you have to force the child at all, you are probably fighting the child's interests. Pushing a youngster to learn too early often causes resentment and sometimes emotional problems. The child may develop a feeling that the parent is more interested in forcing an idea on him than in permitting him to enjoy the activity for the fun of it. Listen to the child. Be interested in many things yourself. Look for ideas, interests, clues—then step gingerly. Always be ready to pull back. Once a child is ready and interested, he will learn very quickly. Creating a stimulating environment is more important than pushing an idea.

Children Learn from Adults

Children begin life with complete dependency on adult judgment. If everything is always planned for them and if adults always present them with solutions for all their problems, they will have little desire to test their own solutions or opportunity to learn how to suspend judgment. Teaching children to test solutions and to postpone judgment is difficult, for these abilities involve thinking abstractly and holding ideas in mind. Most children (adults too) want quick and easy answers and have not learned how to test out solutions to see if they are really right. Many statements are made and accepted with only superficial reasoning to support them and, in most cases, without any firm evidence.

In their studies of critical thinking, psychologists and educators have found that some children have an almost totally negative critical attitude and refuse to accept anything new while others accept almost everything on blind faith alone. To be able to evaluate properly what one hears, sees, or reads, the individual must have the ability, if necessary, to suspend judgment until he has gathered additional information, and then to base an opinion on the objective evidence he has found. This sounds like a lot for a young child to do, but there is evidence that some children are able to do this at an early age. For example, when a child begins to notice differences between his abilities and those of others, and then to choose a game in which he excels, he has critically evaluated a situation based upon the evidence and has formed an objective conclusion that he has acted upon. Children evaluate their parents and will choose one to ask for one thing and another to ask for something else—or sometimes they play one parent off against the other to get what they want.

Unfortunately, most adults become defensive when

they are asked about what they do in their everyday lives and in their jobs, what they have accomplished, of what benefit their actions are to society. Even those who appear to be the most secure become irritated when questioned too closely about why they do certain things the way they do. They find it difficult to evaluate their own actions and motives. As we parents try to teach our youngsters to think critically and effectively, we must be willing to analyze our own behavior. We have to be secure enough to admit that our actions might not be wholly correct in some situations, and even that we are completely wrong in some instances.

Parents set themselves a difficult task when they encourage children to be certain of their statements and to indicate what evidence is needed. It takes a long, tedious effort to teach them to be critical without being cruel or negative and to help them feel secure in postponing judgment until they have had an opportunity to gather all the facts.

"Mom, I can't get the door to close." "I can't get down." "The paste jar won't open." "I can't read this word." If your reaction to any of these statements is a mad dash to the rescue, you are probably losing an opportunity to give your child experience in solving his own problems. "Let me try it." "I can do it." "I can take care of that." "Don't worry, that's easy." Such expressions indicate self-confidence (although sometimes with poor understanding) and a willingness to try. We must stand by to help, but we must keep from jumping in too fast. Unless it's an emergency, delay your response when a child asks for help, and give him a chance to work out a solution. And don't interfere at all when help is not asked, even though the child seems to be floundering a little. Although his solution may not be the best one, it is his.

Thinking Out Loud

We are constantly faced with situations that require that we solve a problem, direct our attention toward a goal, or evaluate a situation to determine what our action should be. What shall we have for supper? Should we patch a pair of pants or are they beyond repair? Shall we take work home tonight, or can it wait to be done in the office tomorrow? How do we find certain information we're interested in? What type of camera shall I purchase? Is it true what the repairman said about the motor in the washing machine? How can I decide?

Most of the time we find solutions to everyday problems such as these without being conscious of weighing ideas, proceeding through evidence, testing hypotheses, and then arriving at a decision. If we are not even conscious of those steps, how can we expect a young child to be aware of what is going on in his parents' minds? "Thinking out loud" is an excellent way to help children learn to evaluate the various factors in a situation.

"Let's see now, what do we have to take along for the picnic?" says Mother to the rest of the family.

"Do we have enough sandwiches, Mother?" says one of the children. "Do we have anything cold to drink? Also, how about a blanket to sit on?"

"If we're going swimming, we can't forget our bathing suits and towels," shouts another.

"Let's see," says Mother. "Do I need to take something cold for us to drink? We could take something cold from the refrigerator, but there's a place in the park that sells cold soda. Since we don't have too much space in our little cooler, maybe it would be better to buy the soda when we get there. What do you think?"

"I think that's a good idea," chimes in one of the youngsters. "Then we can choose what flavor soda we want."

"We could all have different ones," says another.

"Right," says Mother. "That's what we'll do. We'll buy our cold drinks when we get there." There are many opportunities for parents to think out loud and for children to contribute to family decisions.

Sometimes a child who is encouraged to question, evaluate, and come up with original and imaginative ideas at home is ridiculed both by teachers and by other children. It is up to the parents to support the child in such a situation. Too often, busy and harassed teachers are annoyed by original and imaginative students, but children who have been taught to think effectively must also be taught to understand others who, unfortunately, do not have the same ideas.

THE MEANS ARE MORE IMPORTANT THAN THE END

When we are dealing with children, we must be aware that there are many situations in which we need not be concerned about the final solution or the end product. When parents emphasize the end product rather than the processes involved in reaching it, *children erroneously conclude that the product is the only important thing in any given situation.* "That's the *right* answer." "Isn't that a *pretty* picture?" "Let me see what you *made*." "How many did you *finish*?" These questions—and many more—are used over and over again by parents and teachers.

We should not be particularly concerned with what is "good" or "accepted" thinking or how to make sure the thinking always produces the "right" answers. We should be more interested in giving children experiences that help keep their curiosity alive—ones that encourage them to evaluate their environment, to think about problems, and to come up with creative solutions. *At this time, the process is more important than the answer.*

Many of us are used to looking for *the* single answer to a problem situation. As an example, consider those TV programs that almost always show only one solution to a problem; a character is *either* bad or good, never a little of both. In school teachers usually ask for *the* single right answer; tests require *one* choice. In contrast to this approach, we have noted that children who learn to think effectively do better when they are taught to produce several possible correct solutions. Children can be helped to learn that often there are many answers to problems. Children who are imaginative and creative are able to hold at one time several ideas that to a logical adult may seem to be contradictory. We need to be careful that we do not continually judge their thinking and actions by our adult standards, and so frustrate or criticize their attempts.

THE ROLE OF THE SCHOOLS

Schools in the United States today are, as a whole, *vastly* superior to those of former years and to those in any other country. People who are really familiar with the broad base of education in the United States are convinced that the quality of American education is better today than it ever was. This is true even though some critics have shown other national school programs to have a superior system in relation to *one* narrow aspect of education. While our critics are studying other systems and suggesting ways in which we should change, members of foreign educational systems come here to study our programs, and then go home to make every effort to change their own programs so that they will be more like ours. (Ironically, the techniques that are most often criticized in our country are the ones most likely to be adopted by other countries.) While our system is, indeed, comparatively good, there is still a great deal of room for improvement. It has been said that it would take fifty years to change teaching to follow the psychological principles that we now know.

Some Negative Trends

Despite the high quality of American education generally, there are certain worrisome trends that need to be watched very carefully.

(1) There is increasing emphasis on academic skills; parents and teachers tend to be concerned primarily with what is measurable. The examinations for entrance to college

determine the high school curriculum, and this, in turn, determines the elementary school curriculum. The emphasis is on facts rather than on learning. Teachers need to learn how to teach for effective thinking and parents must support this effort.

(2) There is a great deal of pressure to move more difficult material down to lower grades, to increase the number of hours in school, and to give more homework—in general, to make school more demanding. Parents and teachers should resist this pressure. Parents who are enamored of the idea that their children can learn to read a few months earlier must be made aware of the emotional problems that this pressure can bring and of how little gain there is in the long run (even if the program is successful). Many school problems are caused by this early pressure, and many children hate school because of it.

(3) Although there is a new interest on the part of both parents and teachers in how to teach children to think effectively, there is little material to use. Many of the new revisions of textbooks and workbooks use the word "discovery," but they are not really using this technique. The old texts have simply been retitled. New material is too often taught with ancient techniques and becomes a prisoner of these old methods. Teachers need to feel free to try new techniques based on sound learning principles.

(4) Most school budgets are inadequate. Salaries are usually too low to attract creative teachers. Classes are too large. It is difficult to teach effective thinking where there is only one teacher for each twenty children. Larger numbers make the situation almost impossible. There are insufficient funds for trips, equipment, teacher aids, library services, and so forth. If the school is to be a center for teaching children how to learn rather than a factory for the infusion of facts, drastic changes must be wrought.

Educating children is a complicated task, and the vast majority of our citizens do not understand what makes an educational program good. We have all heard about the "panacea boys," with their one magic solution, one answer for all children and all school problems. Although some of the suggestions by these "helpers" have some merit for some children, the suggestions must be considered as part of a total educational program that takes all children into account.

What Needs to Be Done

There are, however, some steps that interested parents can take. Parents can:

(1) Demand that modern school buildings be built. These would not be of the cheesebox variety but would take into account the newer approaches that call for multiple-use areas and rooms of varying size. We are fifty years behind in using our knowledge about building schools, although modern schools cost no more than the outmoded ones.

(2) See that people who are interested in a creative school environment, rather than conservative budget cutters, are elected to boards of education.

(3) See that the board of education employs a dynamic, growing, experimental superintendent, for the strength of the superintendent is the strength of the whole system. A study in New York State showed that the superintendent was the *key* person in making a school system attractive to creative teachers.

(4) Advocate and fight for the highest salaries for teachers. Although money isn't everything, a high salary attracts more applicants and the school can select the best.

(5) Vote for sufficient funds for special services (remedial reading teachers, guidance personnel, etc.). A school system that spends less than $600 per pupil per year is only beginning to meet the most fundamental needs of a program that will teach children to think. Most people are willing to take on tremendous burdens to put their children through college but are unwilling to pay the much smaller yearly cost of preparing them properly for college.

Most communities have exactly the type of school

program that the citizens are interested in having and are willing to pay for. Too many people who preach good education want to indulge a champagne taste on a beer budget.

In any event, parents should be aware of what is going on in school and should attempt to expand on these experiences in a creative manner. Find out what the children are learning, and help them to think effectively using the information that they learn. Supplement the school program wherever you can.

Until society really accepts the importance of teaching children to think, the schools—which reflect the wishes of the community—will not change much in this respect. Therefore, the home remains the most important factor in keeping curiosity, imagination, and creativity alive.

SPECIFIC ACTIVITIES

Before presenting any specific experiences and activities, I would like to discuss the proper environment. This includes the places, the things, and the ideas.

Providing the Places

The places in which curiosity and imagination thrive are everywhere—the apartment or house, the street or back yard, the supermarket, the discount store, the playground, and all the other places all around us. Each of them can provide creative experiences for curious youngsters. "Do cows give cheese and milk, too? How do they get things to grow in cans, Mommy?'' asks Jimmy as he follows his mother in the supermarket. ''Do they give you new clothes?'' asks Billy at the cleaners. ''How do they grow bread?'' he asks in the bakery. ''Is there lots of gasoline in that pump?'' he queries while stopping off for gas.

Parents can help by providing safe play areas that place as few restrictions as possible on the child's actions. Too often one hears, ''Don't get your pants dirty,'' ''Don't throw things on the floor,'' ''Hold the paint brush the right way,'' ''Watch out for the rug,'' ''Don't spill the water.'' Parents who must always have every room in the house neat and clean have probably gone a long way toward extinguishing the behavior we hope to keep alive. There should be at least one room, or area, where the child feels free to experiment.

The back yard in suburban or rural areas also serves children as a laboratory. Yards full of grass, plants, and bushes carefully manicured are not particularly conducive to imaginative and exploratory involvement. An area where children can run, play hide and seek, or roll and tumble makes more sense. The grass may not grow as well and your yard may not look like the pictures in some magazines, but it will be well worth the sacrifice. In the city, the street with its stores, people, and parks can serve as the learning laboratory.

Providing the Things

Some homes have nothing that children are really allowed to play with, while others have such a superabundance of toys, books, and other materials that children hop from one to another, do not know what to choose, and are frustrated looking for what they want. Those with the overwhelming number of toys, books, and other materials are usually middle- and upper-class homes that are oriented toward children and education. Unfortunately, in too many instances the parents give the children all these things so that they will not have to relate to them or spend time with them. ''Go play with your toys." "Don't bother me now." "Go outside and play." "I'll buy you a nice toy if you leave me alone."

A most important element in children's learning to think effectively is the participation of parents in many of their activities and experiences. Having a great many toys and materials is not inherently bad; more important is how the situation is managed. Some parents put many of the toys away and change those that are out when the child becomes bored. They also bring some things out at the child's request. Parents should carefully choose all toys and materials, always asking themselves if these will stimulate the child's imagination, if they are on his level of understanding, and if he will enjoy them over and over again.

Children have always expressed an interest in living things. A pet of some kind teaches many important concepts. Even a fish or a bird can mean a great deal to a child.

Providing the Ideas, the Experiences, and the Challenges

It is important for children to be involved in plans that the family is making. Children's ideas should be discussed fully and taken into account when decisions are made. Children should be asked to contribute their ideas when Father is ready to repair something (or have it repaired), when Mother is thinking about what to prepare for a meal, when the family is deciding where to go, when clothes are being bought, when use of spare money is discussed, or when a large purchase is being considered. *Praise from parents and others when a child thinks of an idea is one of the most important factors in the child's continuing thought development.*

Trips to interesting places provide an important means of challenging children. With *each* visit to the beach, the museum, the zoo, children find *new* ideas, gain *new* insights, and build *new* concepts.

Games also provide learning experiences for children. Some games help children verbalize their ideas and gain a better understanding of things around them. Games can help stimulate awareness, improve memory, and introduce methods of problem solving.

The attitude of adults toward thinking is a central factor in helping children learn to think effectively. There are, however, a number of other qualities, techniques, and abilities that are essential to curiosity and imagination:

Concentration

Creative imagination

Accuracy in observation

Sensitivity to surroundings, perceptions, feelings

A growing vocabulary

Collecting and organizing information, abstracting, discriminating, integrating

A retentive memory

Sensitivity to *associations* between things and ideas, inferences, generalizing

Comparing and evaluating, making judgments, analyzing, clarifying, summarizing

Looking for and finding assumptions, finding and/or making hypotheses

Logical reasoning, interpretation, testing

Independent planning

Self-analysis (ability to see what one has contributed to an idea, to see the emotions and prejudices that may be involved)

Suspending judgment until all the evidence is in

Flexibility—openness (being able to change direction, accept new ideas, admit failure)

Persistence

Analysis of experience

Independent decision making

Specific Activities, Games, Trips, and Ideas

The activities and ideas in the tables that follow (pp. 99–123) are categorized in terms of the *main* goals, although there are often many additional benefits to be derived from each activity. We have focused only on the main goals so that they can be kept clearly in mind by the parent. Though the age range suggests that a child would enjoy a particular activity at a particular age, there is no reason why it cannot be used either earlier or later if the child is interested. Any of these activities and games should be presented in a relaxed fun fashion, for time is on your side and children learn when they are ready. Unlike a classroom situation, there should be no examinations at the end—just the satisfaction and rewards that parents get from watching and listening to the things their children do and say.

Look for natural solutions. Don't make a ritual out of what you do—unless you are sure the child enjoys it—because rituals are often boring. Change activities frequently; then repeat them if the child asks. It is important to find out the child's interest and to modify the activity accordingly. Don't get too finicky about the responses. Remember, the process is more important than the answer. Make a correction if the response is wrong; then forget about it. Take it easy and go slowly. Have fun.

Equipment

Age of Interest	Equipment	Major Goals
All ages	Building blocks (large and small)	Creative imagination
2	Paints and easel	Creative imagination Sensitivity to surroundings —perceptions— feelings Independent planning
2	Children's-size table and chairs	Creative imagination Accuracy in observation— noting detail Sensitivity to *associations* between things and ideas—inferences— generalizing Independent planning
2	Box full of colored cloth and paper, buttons, pipe cleaners, play money	Concentration Creative imagination Flexibility—openness
2	Large crates, boards, cardboard cartons	Creative imagination Independent planning Flexibility—openness
2	Bicycles and wagons	Creative imagination Flexibility—openness
2	A box of old clothes for dress-up fun	Creative imagination Accuracy in observation— noting detail Sensitivity to *associations* between things and ideas—inferences— generalizing

Age of Interest	Equipment	Major Goals

3	An outdoor playhouse	Creative imagination
		Sensitivity to surroundings
		    —perceptions—
		    feelings
		A retentive memory
		Independent planning

4	Put-together toys (building sets, Erector sets, etc.)	Concentration Creative imagination Logical reasoning—inter- pretation—testing Independent planning Flexibility—openness Persistence
4	Materials for making papier-mâché	Concentration Creative imagination Flexibility—openness
5	Ceramic tile and paste for designs	Concentration Creative imagination Flexibility—openness
All ages	Picture books—stress the value and care of books; read books yourself	Concentration A growing vocabulary A retentive memory
All ages	Crayons and paper	Creative imagination Accuracy in observation— noting detail

All ages	Children's records (music
	and storytelling)
		Concentration
		Creative imagination
		Sensitivity to surroundings
		    —perceptions—
		    feelings

Activities

Age of Interest	Activities	Major Goals
3	Imagine a change in a part of the body and ask children what would happen. (E.g., what can you do with four hands that you cannot do with two? Hug twice as hard.)	Creative imagination Sensitivity to *associations* between things and ideas—inferences—generalizing Flexibility—openness
4	Ask children to draw a picture of an animal that does not live on this planet and explain how it lives.	Creative imagination Sensitivity to surroundings —perceptions—feelings Logical reasoning—interpretation—testing
2	Ask children to tell you what an object is and what it does (e.g., spoon, picture, puzzle).	Accuracy in observation—noting detail A growing vocabulary Comparing and evaluating —making judgments —analyzing—critical evaluation—clarifying —summarizing Analysis of experience
3	Tell children to look around for one minute, then to close their eyes and tell what they saw.	Concentration Accuracy in observation—noting detail
4	Ask children to name things that can fly, parts of a car, things that are red, etc.	Creative imagination A growing vocabulary Sensitivity to *associations* between things and ideas—inferences—generalizing

Age of Interest	Activities	Major Goals
4	Ask children to describe something without looking at it.	Accuracy in observation—noting detail A retentive memory
2	Ask children what they would wish for if they could have one wish. What would be the consequences if the wish came true?	Creative imagination Collecting and organizing information—abstracting—discriminating—integrating Comparing and evaluating—making judgments—clarifying—summarizing
5	Tell children to learn about two, three, four, or five new things and tell you about them tomorrow.	Sensitivity to surroundings—perceptions—feelings A retentive memory Analysis of experience
5	Ask children to find new uses for things like pencils and paper clips. Encourage silly ideas, imaginative uses.	Creative imagination Looking for and finding assumptions—making hypotheses Flexibility—openness
6	Encourage children to make up a code and write messages to you and their friends.	Concentration Sensitivity to *associations* between things and ideas—inferences—generalizing Persistence
3	Tell a story without an ending. Ask children to make up several endings.	Creative imagination Looking for and finding assumptions—making hypotheses Logical reasoning—interpretation—testing

Age of Interest	Activities	Major Goals
3	Show children a picture. Ask them to make up a story that would use this picture to illustrate it.	Creative imagination Logical reasoning—interpretation—testing Flexibility—openness
2	Suggest that some letters remind you of animals. Ask children to pick a letter and tell what animals it makes them think of.	Creative imagination Sensitivity to *associations* between things and ideas—inferences—generalizing Flexibility—openness
4	Build something together.	Comparing and evaluating—making judgments—analyzing—critical evaluation—clarifying—summarizing Persistence Analysis of experience
4	Have children keep notebooks of things they would like to do and places they want to visit. Plan and carry out some of the projects.	Independent planning Independent decision making
6	Present children with a real problem that you have. Try out some of their solutions so that they can learn how to test their ideas.	Comparing and evaluating—making judgments—analyzing—critical evaluation—clarifying—summarizing Looking for and finding assumptions—making hypotheses Suspending judgment and conclusions Independent decision making

Age of Interest	Activities	Major Goals
3	Have children plan a party for family or friends. Accept suggestions and help them analyze the consequences of their suggestions.	Independent planning Suspending judgment and conclusions Analysis of experience Independent decision making
4	Think through some problems and suggest hypotheses. Ask children to comment on them. Do they understand how and why you arrived at the conclusion?	A growing vocabulary Comparing and evaluating —making judgments —analyzing—critical evaluation—clarifying —summarizing Analysis of experience
1	Tell the same story over and over again. It strengthens the child's concepts. Talk about it. Examine it from different angles. Find new nuances in its meaning.	Concentration A growing vocabulary
5	Use reference books to find information. Help children learn to do the same. Do it together.	Collecting and organizing information—abstracting—discriminating—integrating Sensitivity to *associations* between things and ideas—inferences—generalizing

Age of Interest	Activities	Major Goals
2	Make trips and visits. Go to a zoo, farm, museum, fair, building, lake, ocean, fish hatchery, to watch construction of a house, a bridge, an airport, etc. Plan trips with children, check their observations and evaluate them afterwards.	Sensitivity to surroundings —perceptions— feelings Collecting and organizing information—abstracting—discriminating— integrating Analysis of experience
3	Discuss events with children, help them understand why things happen.	Accuracy in observation— noting detail Sensitivity to surroundings —perceptions— feelings Sensitivity to *associations* between things and ideas—inferences— generalizing Logical reasoning—interpretation—testing
4	Have children express their ideas verbally, in drawings, with puppets, etc. Ask for topics they would like to talk about or act out.	Creative imagination Accuracy in observation— noting detail Self-analysis
4	Check children's understanding of words they use and ones that you use. Ask them to use words in a new way.	A growing vocabulary A retentive memory

Age of Interest	Activities	Major Goals
4	Look for problems that children suggest overtly or covertly. Work them through, using informal methods. The process is more important than the conclusion. Problems should not be too easy or too difficult. Try to sense balance between these two extremes.	Sensitivity to *associations* between things and ideas—inferences— generalizing Comparing and evaluating —making judgments —analyzing—critical evaluation—clarifying —summarizing Looking for and finding assumptions—making hypotheses Logical reasoning—inter- pretation—testing
3	Draw a few random lines on a page and have a child make as many things out of them as he can.	Creative imagination Flexibility—openness
4	Ask children what they would have to do with an object to make it run, fly, etc.	Creative imagination Accuracy in observation— noting detail Flexibility—openness
3	Ask children what they would be able to do if they were something different (e.g., a giant, an ant).	Creative imagination Sensitivity to *associations* between things and ideas—inferences— generalizing Flexibility—openness
3	Ask children what would happen if they could do something they are not actually able to do (e.g., fly, live underwater).	Creative imagination Sensitivity to *associations* between things and ideas—inferences— generalizing

Age of Interest	Activities	Major Goals
3	Ask children what names they can think of for a picture, a story, etc.	Creative imagination Accuracy in observation— noting detail Sensitivity to *associations* between things and ideas—inferences— generalizing
4	Ask children what new names they can think of for things that are already named (e.g., couch, bread).	Creative imagination Flexibility—openness
6	Ask children to give you an example of a problem children and grownups might have in common. Discuss basis of problem, solution.	Sensitivity to surroundings —perceptions— feelings Collecting and organizing information—abstract- ing—discriminating— integrating Comparing and evaluating —making judgments —analyzing—critical evaluation—clarifying —summarizing Logical reasoning—inter- pretation—testing Analysis of experience
5	Ask for opinions of situations, discuss them, look for alternative solu- tions (e.g., why did your friend cry? All the chil- dren teased him, he was lost).	Collecting and organizing information—abstract- ing—discriminating— integrating Comparing and evaluating —making judgments —analyzing—critical evaluation—clarifying —summarizing Looking for and finding assumptions—making hypotheses Suspending judgment and conclusions

Activities *(Continued)*

Age of Interest	Activities	Major Goals
5	Ask children to describe how they might help a friend with a problem (e.g., no one likes him).	Sensitivity to surroundings —perceptions— feelings Collecting and organizing information—abstracting—discriminating—integrating Comparing and evaluating —making judgments —analyzing—critical evaluation—clarifying —summarizing Looking for and finding assumptions—making hypotheses Logical reasoning—interpretation—testing
3	Give children paper to cut into several shapes (circles, triangles, etc.). Ask them to use these in a drawing or collage in as many ways as possible.	Concentration Creative imagination Flexibility—openness
5	Give a picture to children. Tell them to ask as many questions as possible about the picture.	Accuracy in observation— noting detail Looking for and finding assumptions—making hypotheses
5	Ask children to imagine a well-known thing functioning as something else (e.g., a door as a wagon). Test it.	Creative imagination Looking for and finding assumptions—making hypotheses Suspending judgment and conclusions

Age of Interest	Activities	Major Goals
6	Ask children how they might learn if there were no schools.	Creative imagination Sensitivity to *associations* between things and ideas—inferences—generalizing Comparing and evaluating —analyzing—critical evaluation—clarifying —summarizing
5	Set up frustrating situations. Ask children to deal with them and test the solutions if possible (e.g., a friend left his lunch money at home; a friend got sick on the day of a special trip).	Collecting and organizing information—abstracting—discriminating—integrating Comparing and evaluating —making judgments —analyzing—critical evaluation—clarifying —summarizing Looking for and finding assumptions—making hypotheses Analysis of experience
6	Ask children to make up an unusual story based on a false premise but told logically (e.g., the day the man fell up; the day a man from outer space visited you; the day you could read other people's minds).	Creative imagination Logical reasoning—interpretation—testing Flexibility—openness
5	Make up solutions or conclusions. Ask children to give you problems that could have resulted in the solutions (e.g., the house was torn down, he gave all his money away, he ate only spinach).	Creative imagination Comparing and evaluating —making judgments —analyzing—critical evaluation—clarifying —summarizing Logical reasoning—interpretation—testing

Age of Interest	Activities	Major Goals
4	Give the beginning and end of a story. Have children fill in the middle.	A growing vocabulary A retentive memory Sensitivity to *associations* between things and ideas—inferences—generalizing
5	Ask children to write a song, a poem, a play, a story, make up a dance.	Concentration A growing vocabulary Independent planning
6	Discuss the rules of a game. Ask children to figure out improvements that would create interesting changes in the game. Use games children are familiar with.	Creative imagination Looking for and finding assumptions—making hypotheses Flexibility—openness
5	Make models of things with children (boats, planes, etc.).	Concentration Accuracy in observation—noting detail Persistence
6	Ask children to find a problem that requires a solution and then to invent something that eliminates the problem.	Creative imagination Sensitivity to surroundings—perceptions—feelings Comparing and evaluating—making judgments—analyzing—critical evaluation—clarifying—summarizing Looking for and finding assumptions—making hypotheses

Age of Interest	Activities	Major Goals
3	Ask children to cut different shapes out of magazines and paste them into designs.	Creative imagination Flexibility—openness
5	Start a collection together, or help the children with a collection. Collect rocks, butterflies, stamps, buttons, match covers, photographs, etc. Let the child decide what to collect.	Concentration Accuracy in observation—noting detail Collecting and organizing information—abstracting—discriminating—integrating
5	Help children learn to ask the right questions and to gather evidence. Present a situation (e.g., the man was hurt). Have children ask three or four questions to bring out the whole story.	Sensitivity to surroundings—perceptions—feelings Sensitivity to *associations* between things and ideas—inferences—generalizing Comparing and evaluating—making judgments—analyzing—critical evaluation—clarifying—summarizing Looking for and finding assumptions—making hypotheses Logical reasoning—interpretation—testing
6	Ask children how to do something difficult (e.g., paint the top of a flagpole or a steeple, measure the height of a building with a one-foot ruler, or mount a horse without saddle and stirrups).	Creative imagination Comparing and evaluating—making judgments—analyzing—critical evaluation—clarifying—summarizing Flexibility—openness

Age of Interest	Activities	Major Goals
6	Ask children what they would do in a certain situation (e.g., they ran out of food in a forest, no water came out of the kitchen tap, or a bear walked into your house).	Creative imagination Collecting and organizing information—abstracting—discriminating—integrating Comparing and evaluating —making judgments —analyzing—critical evaluation—clarifying —summarizing Looking for and finding assumptions—making hypotheses
6	Read an interesting and comprehensible newspaper story to children. Ask which parts are based on evidence, which on the reporter's opinion.	Comparing and evaluating —making judgments —analyzing—critical evaluation—clarifying —summarizing Looking for and finding assumptions—making hypotheses Logical reasoning—interpretation—testing Suspending judgment and conclusions
7	Occasionally ask children questions as they make statements. Frame each question carefully, for the response will depend upon how important the child thinks the question is. Ask what the statement is based on.	Looking for and finding assumptions—making hypotheses Self-analysis Suspending judgment and conclusions

Age of Interest	Activities	Major Goals
4	Watch birds together, and try to identify them. Build bird feeders, bird houses, etc.	Sensitivity to surroundings —perceptions— feelings Collecting and organizing information—abstracting—discriminating—integrating Independent planning
3	Read a children's poem and ask the children what it makes them think of.	Concentration Creative imagination Sensitivity to surroundings —perceptions— feelings
4	Ask children to draw a picture on a large piece of wrapping paper. Encourage them to bring together a number of ideas by discussing what they want to draw.	Creative imagination Accuracy in observation— noting detail Sensitivity to *associations* between things and ideas—inferences— generalizing Independent planning
4	Have children read or tell a story. Ask how they might change it.	Creative imagination A growing vocabulary Flexibility—openness
3	Ask children to act like some object (e.g., a tree, a bicycle, a door, a bus).	Creative imagination Accuracy in observation— noting detail Sensitivity to surroundings —perceptions— feelings
4	Take children to see carefully selected films. Watch selected TV programs together. Discuss them.	Accuracy in observation— noting detail Collecting and organizing information—abstracting—discriminating— integrating A retentive memory

Age of Interest	Activities	Major Goals
6	Have unusual and interesting things around the house (e.g., puppet heads, marionettes, papier-mâché animals, plastic dinosaurs, pictures of butterflies, wires, a tiny motor, magnets, a magnifying glass, number games, puzzles). Let children play with them and ask about them. Discuss them when children are interested.	Creative imagination Sensitivity to *associations* between things and ideas—inferences— generalizing Comparing and evaluating —making judgments —analyzing—critical evaluation—clarifying —summarizing Analysis of experience
5	When a child asks a question, encourage him to find out what motivated it.	Self-analysis Analysis of experience
2	Move into areas that are new for you as well as the children. Learn together.	Accuracy in observation— noting detail Sensitivity to surroundings —perceptions— feelings A growing vocabulary
4	Point out something you find in a newspaper or magazine that you think the children might be interested in. If they get involved, continue; if not, drop it. Try again with something else.	A growing vocabulary Collecting and organizing information—abstracting—discriminating— integrating Analysis of experience
3	Listen to records and dramas together. Dramatize, sing, and dance.	Creative imagination Sensitivity to surroundings —perceptions— feelings Flexibility—openness

Age of Interest	Activities	Major Goals
3	Explore together. Take a walk in a park, visit a new part of town, etc.	Accuracy in observation— noting detail Sensitivity to surroundings —perceptions— feelings A growing vocabulary
5	Play games that challenge the child's imagination and his ability to think (checkers, chess, twenty questions, charades, etc.).	Concentration Creative imagination A retentive memory
6	Ask children to estimate distance. Pace off the distance to check their answers.	Accuracy in observation— noting detail A retentive memory
6	Plan and go on a camping trip. Let children camp out in back yard at night. Let them use their own initiative.	Independent planning Analysis of experience Independent decision making
5	List a group of objects. Ask children to find a common quality (e.g., tree, squirrel, ant, plant, fish are all alive).	Collecting and organizing information—abstracting—discriminating— integrating Sensitivity to *associations* between things and ideas—inferences— generalizing Comparing and evaluating —making judgments —analyzing—critical evaluation—clarifying —summarizing

Age of Interest	Activities	Major Goals
4	List a group of objects. Ask children to make up a story using all the objects that you have placed in a bag. This is called ''paper-bag dramatics.''	Creative imagination Logical reasoning—interpretation—testing Flexibility—openness
4	Have a treasure hunt. Bury a treasure and make up a set of interesting clues (e.g., the next clue is a thing that has four legs but does not walk).	Accuracy in observation—noting detail Comparing and evaluating—making judgments—analyzing—critical evaluation—clarifying—summarizing Independent planning
5	Encourage children to plan a play. Let them choose story and characters. Help them only when necessary.	Creative imagination Independent planning Persistence
4	Have a party. Have children make costumes out of scraps of paper and material. Give a prize for the funniest, loudest, cleverest, and prettiest costumes.	Creative imagination Sensitivity to *associations* between things and ideas—inferences—generalizing Flexibility—openness
5	Have children make up new words to old songs they know. Write them down.	A growing vocabulary A retentive memory Flexibility—openness
3	Have children make funny masks from paper bags. Let them give the characters names.	Creative imagination A retentive memory

Age of Interest	Activities	Major Goals

6	Take children on an imaginary trip to somewhere—Europe, an island, the moon. Find out interesting things about the places they visit.	A growing vocabulary
		Comparing and evaluating
		  —making judgments
		  —analyzing—critical
		  evaluation—clarifying
		  —summarizing
		Looking for and finding
		  assumptions—making
		  hypotheses

7	Play a game of spelling words backward.	A growing vocabulary A retentive memory

6	Have children make up imaginary news events and act them out.	Creative imagination
		Accuracy in observation—
		  noting detail
		Sensitivity to *associations*
		  between things and
		  ideas—inferences—
		  generalizing

4	Have children compare two objects. Ask about their similarities and differences.	Accuracy in observation—
		  noting detail
		Sensitivity to surroundings
		  —perceptions—
		  feelings
		Comparing and evaluating
		  —making judgments
		  —analyzing—critical
		  evaluation—clarifying
		  —summarizing

4	Have a child describe in detail an experience he has had.	Collecting and organizing
		  information—abstract-
		  ing—discriminating—
		  integrating
		A retentive memory
		Comparing and evaluating
		  —making judgments
		  —analyzing—critical
		  evaluation—clarifying
		  —summarizing

Age of Interest	Activities	Major Goals
5	Play a game of classification. Have child classify things such as animals, plants, cities, sports, musical instruments, articles bought in certain types of stores, holidays, etc. Keep track and keep score.	Accuracy in observation—noting detail A retentive memory Comparing and evaluating —making judgments —analyzing—critical evaluation—clarifying —summarizing
3	Have a child grow a plant.	Sensitivity to surroundings —perceptions— feelings Independent planning Persistence
6	Play a game called "What do you assume?" Make a statement (e.g., child A gets home from school earlier than child B; there is a shortage of water; the store is out of a brand of cereal), and ask what assumptions can be made.	Sensitivity to *associations* between things and ideas—inferences— generalizing Comparing and evaluating —making judgments —analyzing—critical evaluation—clarifying Looking for and finding assumptions—making hypotheses
6	Ask the child to find out all he can about something that interests him (e.g., how a caterpillar becomes a butterfly; what makes a plant grow; how a dress is made). Help the child locate the information.	Concentration Accuracy in observation—noting detail Collecting and organizing information—abstracting—discriminating—integrating

Age of Interest	Activities	Major Goals
5	Have the child describe himself as he sees himself and as he imagines others see him. What evidence does he have for his conclusions?	Sensitivity to surroundings —perceptions— feelings Self-analysis
4	Hum or whistle a song that the children know. Ask them to identify it. Children can do the same thing to parents.	Sensitivity to surroundings —perceptions— feelings A retentive memory
4	The "Right" game: An adult makes a statement, the children say "right" or "wrong" (e.g., driving in the car, Dad says, "I see a green truck." Children say "right" or "wrong").	Accuracy in observation— noting detail Sensitivity to *associations* between things and ideas—inferences— generalizing Comparing and evaluating —making judgments —analyzing—critical evaluation—clarifying —summarizing
3	Ask the child to imagine he is a type of worker. Have him name the tools and/or equipment he would need.	Accuracy in observation— noting detail Collecting and organizing information—abstract- ing—discriminating— integrating Sensitivity to *associations* between things and ideas—inferences— generalizing
4	Play "Let's learn a new word." Pick odd moments to introduce and explain a new word. Try not to make this too routine.	A growing vocabulary A retentive memory

Age of Interest	*Activities*	*Major Goals*
3	Have children think of imaginative and unusual arts-and-crafts media (e.g., have them paint with sawdust or salt: dye it, spread it, paste it).	Creative imagination Flexibility—openness
4	Ask children to look at things along the road—ads, animals, license plates, cars, signs, etc. Have them name them and tell all they can about them. Have the children remember them.	Concentration Accuracy in observation—noting detail Collecting and organizing information—abstracting—discriminating—integrating
4	Have children choose an object and think of as many words as they can to describe it. As a variation, use a descriptive word and have them guess objects that it can apply to.	Accuracy in observation—noting detail A growing vocabulary Sensitivity to *associations* between things and ideas—inferences—generalizing
5	Play Twenty Questions. Children may ask twenty questions to try to guess chosen word by using "coffeepot" instead of the word when asking questions.	A growing vocabulary A retentive memory Sensitivity to *associations* between things and ideas—inferences—generalizing
5	Play "Animal, vegetable, or mineral."	Sensitivity to surroundings—perceptions—feelings A growing vocabulary Comparing and evaluating—making judgments—analyzing—critical evaluation—clarifying—summarizing

Age of Interest	Activities	Major Goals
5	"Categories." Name as many animals, fish, birds, boys' names, etc., as you can that have a "b" in them.	Collecting and organizing information—abstracting—discriminating—integrating A retentive memory Sensitivity to *associations* between things and ideas—inferences—generalizing
5	Have children name as many words beginning with one letter of the alphabet as they can. Have a contest.	A growing vocabulary A retentive memory
5	Find and name an object beginning with each letter of the alphabet.	Accuracy in observation—noting detail A growing vocabulary
4	Be very quiet. Listen to the sounds you hear. Make a list of what they are.	Concentration Accuracy in observation—noting detail Sensitivity to surroundings—perceptions—feelings
4	Make a map of an area. Follow a route, perhaps in a treasure hunt, on the map.	Looking for and finding assumptions—making hypotheses Logical reasoning—interpretation—testing
4	Play card games (Concentration, Hearts, etc.). Play games that require some thought rather than only luck.	Concentration A retentive memory Comparing and evaluating—making judgments—analyzing—critical evaluation—clarifying—summarizing

Age of Interest	Activities	Major Goals
3	Sing rounds. Make them up and act them out.	Creative imagination Persistence
4	"Continuing story." Someone starts the story and each person adds a sentence to it. Start a new story before the old one gets boring. Bring in unusual situations and problems for children to solve during their parts of the story.	Creative imagination Sensitivity to *associations* between things and ideas—inferences—generalizing Logical reasoning—interpretation—testing
3	"Story box." List a group of words and number them. Pick five or six numbers and make up a story using the words chosen. Adapt for little children by reading words to them. You may also put each word on a slip of paper, drop into box, and pick five or six.	Creative imagination A growing vocabulary Flexibility—openness
3	Blindfold someone and see if he can tell what an object is by touch and/or taste and/or smell.	Concentration Accuracy in observation—noting detail A retentive memory
5	Show a picture for a few seconds. Ask what details can be remembered.	Concentration Accuracy in observation—noting detail A retentive memory

Age of Interest	Activities	Major Goals
5	"Memory touch." One player touches something and names it; the second touches that plus something else and names them; the third touches the first, second, and third object, etc., until someone misses.	Concentration Accuracy in observation—noting detail A retentive memory
5	"Toy pantomime." Act out a toy, and ask the others to guess what it is.	Creative imagination Sensitivity to *associations* between things and ideas—inferences—generalizing Flexibility—openness
5	"Observation." Place a group of objects on the table. Keep them covered. Uncover and quickly replace cover. How many objects can be remembered?	Concentration Accuracy in observation—noting detail A retentive memory
5	Encourage children to plan and carry out a carnival or circus. Raise money for a favorite charity.	Independent planning Independent decision making
4	An adult requests a rhyming word for simple two-line poems (e.g., There was a pig quite fat/who didn't wear a _____ ; I saw a chick with an orange bill,/he waddled slowly by the _____ ; I had a friend whose name was Polly./I play all day with her little _____).	Concentration Sensitivity to surroundings —perceptions— feelings A growing vocabulary

BIBLIOGRAPHY

Burton, William H. *The Guidance of Learning Activities*. New York: Appleton-Century-Crofts, 1962. (For teachers.)

Hullfish, Henry Gordon, and Smith, Philip G. *Reflective Thinking: The Method of Education*. New York: Dodd, Mead, 1961.

Meyers, R. E., and Torrance, E. Paul *Invitation to Thinking and Doing*. Minneapolis: Perceptive Publishing Company, 1960. (Includes Teacher's Manual.)

Rasmussen, Margaret, ed. *Play—Children's Business: Guide to Selection of Toys and Games: Infants to Twelve-Year-Olds,* Association for Childhood Education International, Membership Service Bulletin, no. 7A 1962–1963. Washington, D.C.: ACEI, 1963.

Russell, David H. *Children's Thinking*. Waltham, Mass.: Blaisdell, 1956.

Simpson, Ray H. *Improving Teaching-Learning Processes*. New York: McKay, 1953.

Strong, Ruth. *Helping Children Solve Problems*. Chicago: Science Research, 1953.

Wann, Kenneth D.; Dorn, Miriam Selchen; and Liddle, Elizabeth Ann. *Fostering Intellectual Development in Young Children*. New York: Teachers College, 1962.

Ward, Murial. *Young Minds Need Something To Grow On*. New York: Harper & Row, 1957.

Date Due
